BRITISH HISTORY

ANDREW GODSELL

First published as *Legends of British History* 2008.
Wessex Publishing, Hampshire, Britain.

British History published 2018.
Revised Edition 2023.

Copyright © Andrew Godsell

This book is copyright. Display of the front cover image, and quotation of short passages, for comment or review, are permitted. In other circumstances, no part of this publication may be reproduced or transmitted, anywhere in the known (or unknown) universe, in any form or by any means, including photocopying and recording, without express written permission from the author. Such express written permission must also be obtained before any part of the publication is stored in any retrieval system of any nature.

ISBN 9781720175605

Blog andrewgodsell.wordpress.com

Twitter @AndrewGodsell

YouTube Channel Andrew Godsell

Dedicated to my wonderful wife, Debbie Mattingly-Godsell, whose ancestors lived at Mattingley village, in Hampshire, during the Domesday era.

The Author

Andrew Godsell was born during 1964, in Hampshire. His family owned land in the neighbouring county of Wiltshire – four hundred years earlier. After education at a nondescript comprehensive school, and a sixth form college, Andrew did not go to university. He became something in the City, working for a series of banks, while launching a writing career. Following this Andrew has worked as a civil servant and local government officer – he is currently with the National Health Service.

Why Not Trust the Tories? is Andrew's critical analysis of the relevant political party. *The World Cup and International Football 1872-2016* and *Europe United: A History of the European Cup / Champions League* are comprehensive chronicles, while *Planet Football* features biographical sketches of some of the greatest players. *The Life and Diaries of Samuel Pepys* is a study of the amazing diarist. *Obsessive Compulsive Asperger* appeals as an attempt at alternative autobiography. *Alice's Adventures in Fantasyland* is a modern re-telling of a nineteenth century tale. Andrew's writings on diverse subjects have appeared in magazines, an educational textbook, and on several websites. A contribution to textual accuracy led to an acknowledgement of Mr A Godsell in the Penguin Classics edition of *Dracula* by Bram Stoker.

Andrew was interviewed by the BBC at the 1990 World Cup finals, and ITV at the 2006 tournament, but the film probably ended up on the cutting-room floor. Andrew's efforts have won table tennis and disco dancing competitions. He was publicity co-ordinator of Brooce Fans for Fair Ticketing, a campaign against music ticket touting, that attracted media attention. Andrew featured in the book *Twenty Nights to Rock: Touring with the Boss* by Bill Tangen, an American sports writer, and fellow Bruce Springsteen fan. Andrew starred on the BBC's *Weakest Link* (2009), and his political commentary has been broadcast by the BBC (2016) plus Sky (2017).

Contents

Preface	7
1 Albion	9
2 Britannia	14
3 Camelot	25
4 Anglo-Saxon Chronicle	36
5 Domesday Book and Magna Carta	53
6 The Late Middle Ages	63
7 Early Modern Britain	72
8 The Age of Empire	83
9 The Twentieth Century	93
10 A New Millennium	105

Preface

When and where does British history begin? For me it started at Stonehenge, which I visited during the Easter weekend of 1973, aged eight. I remember being captivated by the aura of Stonehenge, with the ancient stones sat in quiet isolation, holding thousands of years of memory. This was a wonderful survival into the current day from our earliest past. I felt the power of history, something which still holds my imagination, half a century later.

The beginning of a new millennium, in the year 2000, prompted a personal assessment of our history, and the start of work on a book. This gradually developed, as the writing was interweaved with other projects. The first edition, *Legends of British History*, was published in 2008. Fifteen years later, here is an expanded version – with a truncated title.

This book attempts to provide a short survey of the nation's history, that is accessible to the general reader. Our story is a constantly evolving process, with ongoing relevance, as individuals interact with events, and understand their place in history. I follow in the footsteps of Samuel Pepys, as somebody writing a regular diary, and working in public service. More than three centuries after the opening of Pepys' journal, on New Years Day 1660, I started my diary on the first day of 1984.

Having enjoyed reading many history books over the years, I mention some favourites in the following text, and take this opportunity to acknowledge the work of their authors. The latter part of the narrative draws upon experience, and observation, of contemporary Britain. As this piece of writing concludes, I continue a journey through British history.

                Andrew Godsell

                Hampshire
                July 11 2023

1 Albion

Britain has been an island, detached from continental Europe, for about eight thousand years. The territory that became Britain was previously part of the European landmass, until rising sea levels, following the Ice Age, brought the separation around 6000 BCE. The recorded history of Britain begins with colonisation by the Romans, a little under two thousand years ago. Prior to this, there is the long, largely obscure, prehistoric period. Very few specific dates for events, or names of individuals, have come down to us from the illiterate series of societies which originally lived in our island. We do not even know whether these people had any names for their land before the Celts, late in the prehistoric era, developed the word Albion.

Most of our knowledge of prehistoric Britain has been pieced together by historians in the modern day, working alongside archaeologists and scientists, with development of Deoxyribonucleic Acid (DNA) testing in recent decades a particular benefit. When Britain became an island, cut off from north west Europe, far to the east another significant movement, but of people rather than geography, was underway. Neolithic people from Anatolia (now Turkey) started to move westwards into Europe, bringing with them the practice of farming. The Neolithic community advanced slowly across many generations, with a group reaching Britain, via Iberia and then France, around 4000 BCE. The relatively sophisticated Neolithic people flourished in Britain, and their numbers grew rapidly, with DNA studies showing that the native hunter-gatherer population mostly died out. Besides farming, which remains a vital part of the contemporary British economy, Neolithic culture featured the building of large stone monuments, known as megaliths.

Near the end of Thomas Hardy's novel *Tess of the D'Urbervilles* (published in 1891), there is a dramatic scene at Stonehenge. Angel Clare, the husband of Tess, remarks that Stonehenge is "Older than the centuries; older than the D'Urbervilles". Besides being far older than any Briton we are able to trace by name, Stonehenge is probably the most unmistakable building – or ruin of a long-lost structure – in Britain. Here is a tangible connection to the people who lived in this island during our prehistory. Work on the site in Wiltshire commenced around 3000 BCE, when an earthwork, comprised of banks and ditches, was built with the use of primitive tools. A construction of this type is known as a henge. The first stones arrived around five hundred years later, with the installation in about 2500 BCE of the bluestones. These were transported from the Preseli Mountains, in the south west of Wales. It is amazing to think that approximately 80 of these stones, weighing up to four tons each, were moved across a distance of 240 miles as far back in time as four and a half thousand years ago. Current thinking suggests the stones were transported using a combination of rollers, sledges, and rafts. As recently as 2021, strong evidence has been put forward that these stones were originally erected as a circle in Wales, around 3400 BCE, before being moved to their present location.

In around 2500 BCE a new group of farmers, known as the Beaker People, arrived in Britain. They originated in eastern Europe, and moved westwards, with the group who reached Britain probably having come from what is now Germany. The Neolithic population was in decline, and within a few centuries the Beaker People made up the vast majority of the inhabitants of Britain. The latter group introduced distinctive pottery, and had a custom of burying their dead with pots in the graves. A notable group of Beaker burials have been found in the area of Stonehenge, and these people continued the development of the site.

The Outer Ring was constructed circa 2000 BCE, using sarsen stones, brought from the Marlborough Downs, about 20 miles north of Stonehenge. The journey was shorter than that taken by the bluestones, but the transportation across land of the sarsen stones, which weighed up to 50 tons each, must have required a monumental effort. At Stonehenge stone lintels were placed on top of the sarsen stones, with these constructs being held in place by powerful joints. Modern theory suggests that a system of levers and ropes was used to manoeuvre the stones into their final positions. Further building, including re-arrangement of the bluestones into what is now the Inner Circle, continued at intervals until around 1600 BCE. Britain had by now moved from the Stone Age into the Bronze Age, the latter of which stretched from about 2200 BCE to 750 BCE. As people learned how to produce bronze, by mixing copper with tin, tools became more sophisticated than in the past. This in turn gave way to the Iron Age, and further improvements, with iron being stronger than bronze. The Iron Age began around 800 BCE, towards the end of the Bronze Age, and lasted until the influence of Roman conquest took Britain into a new era.

Archaeologists and scientists have provided good estimates of the period when Stonehenge was built, and method of construction. It appears, however, that the purpose will always remain a mystery. The most credible suggestions focus on astronomical, or other scientific, purpose. These are based on an alignment of stones with the sun, as dawn breaks on the longest day of the year, which is usually June 21. Other serious contenders advance the idea of Stonehenge as a religious temple, in view of the importance worship has always held in human society. Running alongside this is the possibility that Stonehenge was a burial ground, for the leaders of the people that built this enormous edifice. One of the most commonly-known ideas is that Stonehenge was built by the

Druids. This appears to have originated with John Aubrey (1626-1697), an antiquarian, folklorist, owner of estates in Wiltshire, and author of *Brief Lives* – a collection of biographical sketches of famous men, plus a few women, who lived in the seventeenth century. The theory is probably incorrect, as the Druids used forest temples as places of worship, rather than stone buildings. Nevertheless the modern Druids regularly gather at Stonehenge, for the Summer solstice festival.

The earliest surviving written reference to Stonehenge appears in *History of the English* by Henry of Huntingdon, which dates from around 1130. Henry wrote about "Stanenges, where stones of wonderful size have been erected after the manner of doorways", adding that "no one can conceive how such great stones have been so raised aloft, or why they were built there". Various theorists have advanced alternative cases for the Saxons, Danes, Egyptians, French, or Bronze Age Greeks as builders of Stonehenge, with scholarship being entwined with the fantastical. The most famous of the legendary explanations revolves around the traditions associated with King Arthur. The tale first appears in Geoffrey of Monmouth's *History of the Kings of Britain*, written in about 1136 – a few years after Henry of Huntingdon's work. According to Geoffrey, during the fifth century Hengest, an invading Saxon leader, massacred three hundred British nobles. Aurelius Ambrosius, the British high king, decided to raise a memorial to his fallen supporters, and Merlin, the mentor of Arthur, had the idea of transporting the Giant's Ring stone circle from Ireland. Uther Pendragon, the father of Arthur, led an expedition, during which Merlin used magic to relocate the stones to Britain, whereupon they formed the rings of Stonehenge. The bodies of Aurelius Ambrosius and Uther Pendragon were reputed to have been buried at Stonehenge. Most of this is obviously fiction, but Aurelius Ambrosius gave his name to Amesbury, the town just east of Stonehenge. Salisbury, eight miles to the south of Stonehenge, has been seriously suggested as the site of the Battle of Camlann, in which Arthur suffered a fatal blow, and Guenevere ended her days in a convent at Amesbury.

Stonehenge is among the "Seven Wonders of Britain", an accolade bestowed by a public poll, conducted in 2002. The other wonders are Big Ben, the Eden Project, Hadrian's Wall, the London Eye, Windsor Castle, and York Minster. The enduring importance of Stonehenge contrasts with the transitory nature of the Millennium Dome, built in London to mark the year 2000. The site of the dome was subsequently sold, and redeveloped as the O2 Arena, a concert and sports venue, owned by a telecommunications company, which opened in 2007.

Over the centuries, most of the original Stonehenge has been lost, with stones probably plundered for use in other construction. It was not until

1918 that ownership of Stonehenge transferred to the British government, and conservation became a priority. In 1978 public access to the actual stones, as opposed to the surrounding area, was curtailed. The restrictions have been continued by English Heritage, which has managed the site since 1984, balancing the need to conserve Stonehenge with a wish to make it accessible to the British public, and the many foreign tourists for whom it is a magnet. The work of English Heritage, and similar organisations, such as the National Trust, plays a vital role in preserving the physical presence of history. In parallel, historians maintain and develop our story in written form.

The first known written description of Britain was produced by Pytheas, an explorer from Massalia, then a Greek colony, and now Marseille in France. He visited our island in about 325 BCE, during a navigation of north west Europe. Pytheas mentioned the extensive farming of wheat in Britain, explaining "The natives collect the sheaves in great barns and thrash out the corn there, because they have so little sunshine that an open thrashing-place would be of little use in that land of clouds and rain". As this information was communicated to continental Europe, Britain started to get its reputation as a place with less than ideal weather.

Pytheas recorded that the inhabitants called their territory Albion. He introduced the name Prettanike, which meant a land of painted people, referring to the face paint worn by the Celtic-speaking inhabitants. The term Celt is a modern idea, developed to describe a group of people who arrived from continental Europe, and dominated Britain from around 500 BCE. The earliest of these people whose name has survived is Beli Mawr, who ruled in what is now Wales, and possibly southern England, from about 100 BCE. Beli Mawr was followed as leader by a son, Lud, who is reputed to have rebuilt the city of Trinovantum, which Geoffrey of Monmouth suggests was founded by Brutus, an exile from Troy, and originally named Troia Nova (New Troy). Lud renamed the city Caer Lud (Lud's Fort), and this eventually became the name London.

The Greek word Prettanike evolved into a Latin equivalent, Britannia, the name by which the Romans knew Britain. The island was invaded in the year we now know as 55 BCE, as Julius Caesar led an army of the Roman Republic. This was the dominant state in Europe, having conquered much of the Mediterranean area, and expanded its territory to cover Gaul – the land that is now France. Caesar returned to Albion in 54 BCE, and several British tribes united to fight against the invasion. The British alliance was led by Lud's brother, Caswallon, ruler of the Catuvellauni. Caesar quickly returned to his base in Gaul, faced by rebellion there. Political and trading links between the Romans and Britons were established, with the former very much the stronger force.

Julius Caesar seized power as leader of the Roman Republic in 49 BCE, but was murdered in a coup five years later. Subsequently Caeser's grand nephew, and adopted son, Octavian, ruled as the first Roman Emperor, from 27 BCE until 14 CE.

The earliest name found on a British coin is that of Commius, an ally of Caesar during the latter's incursions. Commius went on to rule the Atrebates – with a territory covering parts of Berkshire, Hampshire, and Wiltshire – and died in about 20 BCE. Commius was not actually British, as he originated from the Belgae, a group of people from Gaul, whose name is recalled in a contemporary state. In 1830, Britain hosted an international conference, which recognised the establishment of Belgium, recently seceded from the Netherlands. This was followed by the Treaty of London, in 1839, by which the Netherlands accepted the new state, and the European powers guaranteed the independence of a neutral Belgium. Seventy five years later, in 1914, the invasion of Belgium by Germany, a signatory of the treaty, led Britain to enter World War One. Moving forward another century, Brussels, the capital city of Belgium, is currently also the effective capital of the European Union – although there are also major EU institutions based at Frankfurt (Germany), Luxembourg City (Luxembourg), and Strasbourg (France).

2 Britannia

Boudicca is one of the most famous British women, despite the limited information available about her life, as the leader of the struggle to retain independence against Roman invaders. Boudicca, probably born around 25 CE, is also recalled as Boadicea, this being the Latin equivalent. The Iceni, who lived in an area now covered by Norfolk, Suffolk, and part of Cambridgeshire, had been one of the peoples that accepted Roman dominance when Julius Caesar led the original invasions. It is not clear whether or not Boudicca was a member of the Iceni, but she appears to have been born into a noble family in one of Britain's tribes. This background led to Boudicca marrying Prasutagus, the king of the Iceni.

The Romans returned to Britain in the year 43, a century after the initial incursions, and set about the conquest of the island, under the leadership of the Emperor Claudius. Prasutagus rapidly accepted the authority of the new invaders, acquiescing to the demand that his territory become a client kingdom. In return for allegiance to the Empire, including the enslavement of many Iceni people, Prasutagus received military and economic support from the Romans. The establishment of clients in some areas, combined with outright conquest in others, enabled the Romans to subdue most of the area that now makes up England within a few years of the invasion of 43, despite the resistance led by Caratacus, the king of the Catuvellauni.

The Iceni maintained a degree of autonomy, from the Romans, through to the death of Prasutagus, which occurred in 60. The king bequeathed a large part of his fortune to Nero, who had succeeded Claudius as Emperor in 54, while also providing generously for Boudicca, and their two daughters – whose names are unknown to us. The intention was that Boudicca would act as a regent until her daughters, who were adolescents, were able to assume control. The Roman leadership in Britannia, their name for Britain, reacted angrily to Prasutagus' intent, seeing the bequest of personal wealth to his family as contrary to their law. Within a few days of the death of Prasutagus, Romans seized land and property from the Iceni, in a savage reprisal. Boudicca was publicly whipped, and her young daughters suffered a worse fate, being raped by Roman soldiers.

Boudicca and her daughters soon regained their freedom, and set about organising a rebellion against the Romans, in which several other tribes joined the Iceni. These included the Trinovantes, whose settlement Camulodunum (now Colchester) had been captured by the Romans in the year 49. Boudicca led a massive army in an attack on Camulodunum, in which all of the Romans there were killed, and the settlement was torched. The Iceni and their allies subsequently marched towards

Londinium – destined to become London. Suetonius Paulinus, the governor of Britannia, hastened back from Wales, where he had ended a separate revolt, with the aim of putting down the Iceni. He decided, however, that he lacked the force to save Londinium, and left its inhabitants to their fate. Boudicca's army repeated the destruction of Camulodunum, as they massacred the Romans of Londinium, and burnt the town to the ground. Boudicca then led the rebel forces, which are reputed to have grown to 200,000 people, from Londinium to Verulamium (now St Albans). The Iceni wished to attack Verulamium, as it was the capital of the territory belonging to their traditional enemy, the Catuvellauni, who had recently found favour with the Romans. With Suetonius Paulinus still feeling unable to combat them, the Iceni and their allies overran Verulamium.

Tacitus records, in *The Annals of Imperial Rome*, that up to 70,000 Romans were killed in the attacks on Camulodunum, Londinium, and Verulamium. Tacitus is our main source of information about Boudicca's rebellion, although it occurred when he was a child. Born in about 55, Tacitus was to marry Julia, daughter of Gnaeus Julius Agricola, the governor of Britannia from 77 to 85. Another important source is the writing of Cassius Dio (circa 155-circa 235), who provided a striking physical description of Boudicca, in *Roman History*:

In stature she was very tall, in appearance most terrifying, in the glance of her eye most fierce, and her voice was harsh. A great mass of the tawniest hair fell to her hips, around her neck was a large golden necklace, and she wore a tunic of diverse colours over which a thick mantle was fastened with a brooch. This was her invariable attire.

There was a real possibility of the revolt defeating the Romans, regaining independence for the people of Britain. Boudicca, however, made a vital mistake, as she hesitated to directly confront the opposing force. Suetonius Paulinas, being the more experienced military commander, took advantage of this lapse, and stationed his forces in a favourable position for the anticipated clash. The Roman army numbered only about 10,000 men, but its unity and experience gave it a good chance of defeating the much larger British army. The site of the encounter has not been established beyond doubt, but Mancetter, in Warwickshire, is the most likely location. The battle appears to have taken place during the year 61, with the revolt having stretched across several months. The families of the British soldiers, including women, children, and the elderly, gathered near the battlefield. Perhaps they wished to cheer their comrades on to victory, or maybe felt proximity to the British army was the best protection against a possible Roman onslaught upon the innocent. Ahead of the battle, Boudicca rode among her army on a chariot, and is reputed to have said:

It is not as a woman descended from noble ancestry, but as one of the people that I am avenging lost freedom, my scourged body, the outraged chastity of my daughters. Roman lust has gone so far that not our very person, nor even age or virginity, are left unpolluted. But heaven is on the side of a righteous vengeance. A legion which dared to fight has perished, the rest are hiding themselves in their camp, or are thinking anxiously of flight. They will not sustain even the din and the shout of so many thousands, much less our charge and our blows. If you weigh well the strength of the armies, and the causes of the war, you will see that in this battle you must conquer or die. This is a woman's resolve.

The battle proved to be a short exchange, in which the technically superior Romans out-witted the British. The first military defeat for the British rebellion proved to be a decisive turning-point. Although some resistance continued, Boudicca ceased to be a leader. The Romans intensified the subjugation of Britain, and the Iceni experienced particularly callous treatment. The client system was retained in other areas, with one of the main beneficiaries being Togidubnus, king of the Regnii, a people who lived in what is now Sussex, Hampshire, and Kent. Support for the Romans offered by Togidubnus, possibly including help in defeating Boudicca, led to his being rewarded with an ornate palace, at Fishbourne, near Chichester, in West Sussex. Remains of the palace were discovered in 1960, and regular excavation has been carried out since then at the site, now a popular museum, maintained by the Sussex Archaeological Society. The surviving structure of the palace includes spectacular mosaic flooring. The grounds of the museum also feature the re-creation of a Roman garden. In the absence of any physical remnants of Boudicca's rebellion, Fishbourne Roman Palace is the outstanding location for those wishing an insight into life in Britain at the start of the occupation.

The fate of Boudicca is not certain. Some accounts suggest she was killed fighting in the decisive battle, but there is also speculation that she escaped death in combat, only to commit suicide, by taking poison, in order to avoid impending vengeance. In the seventeenth century, a legend developed that Boudicca was buried at Stonehenge, reputedly constructed as a monument to her memory. Other stories suggest a burial in London, beneath King's Cross Station, or at Parliament Hill on Hampstead Heath. These possible resting spots are unlikely, given that Boudicca probably died in either the Midlands or East Anglia.

Over the last two centuries Boudicca's significance has increased, through comparisons with Queen Victoria and Margaret Thatcher. Victoria (reigned 1837-1901) was head of the British Empire, which followed that of the Romans among the most powerful in the world. The name Victoria is the modern English equivalent of the Latin Boadicea. A statue of Boudicca, and her daughters, by Thomas Thornycroft, was commissioned by Prince Albert of Saxe-Coburg-Gotha, the husband of Victoria. This statue is currently situated on Victoria Embankment in Westminster, having been moved there in 1902. In the latter part of the twentieth century, Margaret Thatcher's domineering style, as a Conservative Prime Minister, resulted in her frequently being referred to as a latter day Boudicca. Thatcher's rigid defence of (what she perceived to be) British interests, within the European Economic Community, an organisation founded in 1958, on the basis of the Treaty of Rome (agreed the previous year), repeated Boudicca's defiance of the Roman Empire. Boudicca does not feature in the *Anglo-Saxon Chronicle*, as memory of her rebellion had faded when this was written. The lack of British native literature at the start of the first millennium means we owe our knowledge of Boudicca, and the effort to retain national independence, to the accounts written by Roman historians.

Modern estimates suggest the population of Britain was around two million people when the Roman army, of around 40,000 soldiers, arrived in the year 43. Ruthless military activity killed many Britons, probably reducing the number of natives by about a tenth, within half a century. Sextus Julius Frontinus, governor of Britannia from 74 to 77, completed the conquest of Wales. The Romans also wished to extend their Empire northwards, into the land that became Scotland. An invasion began during the year 71, led by Quintus Petillius Cerialis, who had preceded Sextus Julius Frontinus. Gnaeus Julius Agricola succeeded, during his spell as governor, in a concerted effort to gain territory in Scotland, winning a major victory over a native force in the Battle of Mons Graupius, in 84. Agricola was recalled to Rome the following year, and over the next few decades his successors did not actively pursue an attempt to conquer Scotland.

Several decades after the campaign led by Boudicca, there were lingering challenges to Roman rule, by the native Britons. Quintus Pompeius Falco, who had recently become the governor, defeated a rebellion by the Brigantes, a tribe in northern England, during 118. In an attempt to bolster authority, Emperor Hadrian arrived in 122, as part of an extended tour of his territories. Hadrian was the first Roman Emperor to visit Britain since Claudius led the invasion. Hadrian (whose full name was Publius Aelius Hadrianus) was born in Rome in the year 76, and became the adopted son of Trajan, his immediate predecessor as Emperor. Hadrian ruled from 117 until his death in 138, and gave his name to Hadrian's Wall, the most impressive relic of the imperial occupation of Britain. He also features in one of the most famous books written by a British historian, *The History of the Decline and Fall of the Roman Empire* by Edward Gibbon (1737-1794) – published in six volumes between 1776 and 1788. Gibbon wrote that Hadrian's life was:

Almost a perpetual journey; and as he possessed the various talents of the soldier, the statesman, and the scholar, he gratified his curiosity in the discharge of his duty. Careless of the difference of seasons and of climates, he marched on foot, and bareheaded, over the snows of Caledonia, and the sultry plains of the Upper Egypt; nor was there a province of the empire which, in the course of his reign, was not honoured with the presence of the monarch.

Caledonia was the Roman name for the land north of Hadrian's Wall, with the natives being known as the Caledonii. The ancient name Caledonia has survived, as a romanticised identity for Scotland, through to the current day. Britannia, a fictional symbol of British independence, also derives from that era. Ironically Britannia, a seated female figure, is based upon a design used on Roman coins in Britain, from around 119, during the rule of Hadrian. The image of Britannia has regularly been used on British coinage since the reign of Charles II (1660-1685), including it featuring on the 50 pence piece, from 1969 to 2008, followed by the £2 coin, from 2015.

The aim was that Hadrian's Wall should mark the northern boundary of the Empire, supporting defence of Roman territory against possible attacks from Scotland. Work was initially overseen by Aulus Platorius Nepos, who became governor of Britannia in 122, being chosen by Hadrian to replace Quintus Pompeius Falco. There was another change about three years later, with Lucius Trebius Germanus taking the post, but his tenure was also short. The main construction of Hadrian's Wall – largely from local limestone – was completed in about 130. The wall stretched across a distance of 74 miles, from coast to coast – to the south of the current border between England and Scotland. Initially a series of small forts, known as milecastles, were built at intervals of about a mile along the wall. This was followed, a few years later, by the construction of 14 full-sized forts.

With creep into Scotland being revived by the Romans, work on a new boundary, about a hundred miles north of Hadrian's Wall, began in 142. This is known as the Antonine Wall, after Emperor Antoninus Pius (138-161), although he never visited Britain. The Antonine Wall was not completed until 154, and the structure was abandoned by the Roman army in 162, as they retreated to the more secure Hadrian's Wall. The Caledonians in turn breached Hadrian's Wall in 180, and engaged the Romans in military conflict across the northern fringe of Britannia for several years. An uneasy peace was agreed in 184, but there were further attacks from the natives of Scotland, the most significant being quelled in 197.

The Romans established a solid administrative structure, in what is now England and Wales, including an extensive network of roads, used to move people and goods between major towns. Ancient Britons had been constructing rough trackways for centuries, but the new roads were sophisticated, with solid paving. The routes of many such roads, mostly established by the Romans before the end of the second century, continue to be used in contemporary Britain. The settlers had less influence on the variant of Celtic language, called Common Brittonic, spoken in Britain. Common Brittonic remained largely intact, although some Latin words were absorbed from Roman usage, until it was replaced by Old English, introduced by the Anglo-Saxons.

Emperor Septimius Severus, who took power in 193, aimed to conquer Caledonia, personally leading a large army there in 209. He gained territory, through a combination of military action and diplomacy. Cassius Dio records in *Roman History*:

A very witty remark is reported to have been made by the wife of Argentocoxus, a Caledonian, to Julia Augusta. When the empress was jesting with her, after the treaty, about the free intercourse of her sex with men in Britain, she replied: "We fulfil the demands of nature in a much better way than do you Roman women, for we consort openly with the best men, whereas you let yourselves be debauched in secret by the vilest". Such was the retort of the British woman.

Septimius Severus ruled jointly with a son, Caracalla, from 198, and another son, Geta, joined them as a third Co-Emperor in 209. Septimius Severus died in 211, at Eboracum (now York), and his sons agreed a peace with the Caledonians. From this point in time, the Romans did not resume efforts to conquer Scotland. Caracalla and Geta clashed bitterly with each other, until the former had the latter murdered, at the end of 211, following their return to Rome. Caracalla ruled as sole Emperor until he was assassinated, by a disaffected Roman soldier, in 217. The murder occurred at Carrhae – now Harran in Turkey – during a war against the Parthian Empire, based in the land that became Iran. Caracalla had implemented an idea of Septimius Severus, dividing Roman Britain into two provinces, Britannia Superior (the south, nearer to Rome, with London as its capital), and Britannia Inferior (the north, further away, and administered from York).

The Roman Empire experienced a prolonged crisis during the third century, and from 260 to 274 Britain joined Gaul in establishing a breakaway state, now known as the Gallic Empire. The first Gallic Emperor, Postumus, ruled from 260 until 268, at which point he was killed by members of his army. A series of short reigns by other Gallic Emperors followed, until a military defeat by the original Empire in 274. Twelve years later, another revolt was led by Carausius, a naval commander, who declared himself Emperor of Britain and northern Gaul in 286. Carausius reigned until 293, when he was assassinated by Allectus, his treasurer, who in turn took the role of rebel Emperor in Britain. An army loyal to the official Empire, led by Constantius Chlorus and Julius Asclepiodotus, invaded in 296, and Allectus was killed in battle – probably at Silchester, in Hampshire. Britannia Superior was now divided into Britannia Prima and Maxima Caesariensis, while Britannia Inferior split into Britannia Secunda and Flavia Caesariensis. This new division, into four provinces, was part of a major reorganisation of the Roman Empire, ordered by Diocletian (ruled 284-305).

At some point in the third century, Saint Alban, a British Christian, was executed by the Romans. The year of this martyrdom is unclear, but the *Anglo-Saxon Chronicle* placed it in 283. Alban's feast day is June 22, the date on which he is believed to have been killed. Alban lived at Verulamium, the location of a battle in the campaign led by Boudicca. Alban, who was a pagan, provided shelter to a clergyman fleeing Roman persecution of Christians. Inspired by his guest, Alban rapidly converted to Christianity. The process was described by the Venerable Bede (circa 673-735), a monk of Jarrow Priory in Northumbria, and one of the foremost scholars of his day. In the *Ecclesiastical History of the English People*, Bede wrote:

Having observed that his guest spent whole days and nights in continual praying and watching, he felt himself on a sudden inspired by the grace of God, and began to emulate so glorious an example of faith and piety, and being leisurely instructed by his wholesome admonitions, casting off the darkness of idolatry, he became a Christian in all sincerity of heart.

A church and shrine was set up, apparently during the fourth century, at the place where Alban had been executed. In 793 an abbey was built, under the direction of Offa, king of Mercia, near the site of Verulamium, which had now been reduced to ruins. A town subsequently developed, becoming St Albans – this name featured in the Domesday Book of 1086. Paul of Caen, a Norman Abbot of St Albans, set about rebuilding the church during 1077, and work was completed in 1089. The abbey was dissolved in 1539, during Henry VIII's attack on religious houses, and a version of Saint Alban's Shrine, dating from 1308, was wrecked, with his bones being lost. The building survived, in a poor state of repair, until major works were undertaken during the nineteenth century, and it became a cathedral in 1877. The apparent remnants of Saint Alban's Shrine were rebuilt in 1872, and further restoration was followed by rededication in 1993 – in a ceremony attended by Queen Elizabeth, the Queen Mother.

The Emperor Diocletian commenced the "great persecution" of Christians within the Roman Empire, which was continued by Galerius (ruled 305-311). The killing of a Christian named George, at the eastern fringe of the Empire, would ultimately have an influence on England. George appears to have been a Palestinian soldier, born in around 280, who was tortured, and murdered, at Nicomedia – now Izmit in Turkey – on April 23 303. George is the patron saint of England, and the flag of Saint George is a national emblem, but it is almost certain he never visited England. A legend that George sailed through the stretch of water that separates south west England from the southern coast of Ireland – now known as Saint George's Channel – in order to visit Glastonbury, the spiritual home of English Christianity, can be dismissed as wishful fiction.

Saint George's place in the national affections stems from the ironic way in which the English, while often displaying a patriotism that borders on nationalism, with an alleged superiority to other nations, have relied heavily on the assimilation of foreign influences in the development of our history, and culture. George is a saint whom the English have had to share with many other peoples, and places. At various times George has been acclaimed as patron saint of Antioch, Aragon, Armenia, Branganza, Catalonia, Constantinople, Ethiopia, Ferrara, Genoa, Georgia, Germany, Hanover, Hungary, Lithuania, Malta, Portugal, Russia, Schleswig, Valencia, and Venice. George has also been adopted as patron saint by archers, armourers, husbandmen, knights, and soldiers, while his influence is supposed to have helped people suffering from leprosy, plague, and syphilis.

Although Saint George is generally associated with the man murdered in 303, there has been some debate about his original identity. Edward Gibbon, in *The History of the Decline and Fall of the Roman Empire*, asserted that Saint George was the same person as George of Cappadocia, a notoriously corrupt tax collector, who became the Christian Archbishop of Alexandria, and was murdered by a pagan mob in 361. Gibbon wrote that, in the manner of his death, George "assumed the mask of a martyr, a saint, and a Christian hero; and the infamous George of Cappadocia has been transformed into the renowned St George of England, the patron of arms, of chivalry, and of the garter".

The single action for which Saint George has become known is an astounding act of chivalry, in which he rescued a damsel in distress, and slayed a dragon. The popularisation of this tale cannot, however, be traced much further back than the appearance of the *Golden Legend*, a collection of biographies of saints, written by Jacobus de Voragine, an Italian prelate, around 1260. This book was translated into English, in 1483, by William Caxton, the founder of English printing. The yarn has been stretched many times, with many variants, but the basic story can be recounted in a few sentences. A dragon was said to have preyed upon a fabled land, using its vile breath to poison humans. The tale, previously located in Cappadocia, was moved to a place called Silene, in Libya, by Voragine. The people managed to appease the dragon by feeding it two sheep each day, until the supply of these animals was nearly exhausted. A decision was made to start offering humans as food for the dragon, and the drawing of lots selected the king's daughter as the first such victim. The moment of sacrifice impended, but George rescued the princess, using her girdle to capture the monster. George offered to kill the dragon, in return for a community conversion to Christianity. The dispatch of the dragon was celebrated with mass baptisms, following which the residents of Silene lived a Christian life, in honour of George's brave act.

George was canonised in 494, by Pope Gelasius I, as the cult stretched across the Middle East and Europe. Knowledge of George apparently first reached Britain around 670, when Arculf, a Frankish bishop, recounted information to Saint Adomnan, an Irishman who was Abbot of Iona, in Scotland. Adomnan wrote down the detail, which in turn featured in the Venerable Bede's *Martyrology*, during the eighth century – the earliest recorded English reference to Saint George. In the latter part of the Anglo-Saxon era, churches in England started to be named after Saint George, and he featured in *Lives of the Saints*, a book by Aelfric "the Grammarian" – abbot successively of Cerne Abbas (Dorset) and Eynsham (Oxfordshire) – in about 997.

Constantius Chlorus became Roman Emperor, jointly with Galerius, during 305 and – after a spell on the continent – returned to Britain. Constantius died in the following year at Eboracum, and was succeeded as Co-Emperor by his son, Constantine I (306-337). In 330 the city of Byzantium was renamed Constantinople, in honour of Constantine, who decided to make it the capital of the Eastern Roman Empire. Constantius Chlorus married twice, with his first wife, Helena, who was Greek, being the mother of Constantine. After divorcing Helena, Constantius married

Theodora, who appears to have been a daughter of Maximian, the Co-Emperor from 286 to 305 – alongside Diocletian. A definite daughter of Maximian, named Fausta, married Constantine, who had her executed in 326, for apparent disloyalty. The persecution of Christians halted in 312, upon the abrupt conversion to the religion of Constantine I. By the end of the fourth century, Christianity was the leading religion within the Empire.

During a pilgrimage to Jerusalem in 326, Helena, the mother of Constantine, discovered the supposed True Cross, on which Jesus was crucified. A legend developed that Saint Helena, as she is now remembered, was born in Britain, and became the basis of the novel *Helena* by Evelyn Waugh (published in 1950). Saint Helena also gave her name to an island in the Atlantic, which became a British colony in 1658. The remoteness of Saint Helena, more than 1,100 miles off the coast of west Africa, led to it being the location where Napoleon Bonaparte was sent into exile in 1815, remaining there until his death in 1821. In the present day, the islands of Saint Helena, Ascension, and Tristan da Cunha are administratively grouped together, as one of the 14 British Overseas Territories, dotted around the world. These are largely self-governing, but not independent members of the United Nations, with the United Kingdom being responsible for their defence and international relations.

The Caledonians were gradually replaced as the pre-eminent tribe north of Hadrian's Wall by another group, who came to be known by the Romans as the Picts. The name originated from the Latin word "picti", meaning "painted people" – an echo of Pytheas' Prettanike name for Britain. During the fourth century, Britain came under attack by forces from Scotland and Ireland, plus the Saxons of Germany. These Barbarian incursions were particularly strong in 367, 381, and 396. In the latter part of the preceding century, the Romans had established a series of defensive forts along a stretch of coast they called the Saxon Shore – from Norfolk to Hampshire – to counter the threat from Saxons. Remains of one of these forts survive alongside Portchester Castle, a Norman building, near Portsmouth in Hampshire. When Britannia was invaded during 381 by Picts and Scots – the latter of whom lived at that time in Ireland, an island which the Romans knew by the name Hibernia – the attack was defeated by Magnus Maximus, a Roman general. He was proclaimed as a rebel Emperor in Britain during 383, and also conquered Gaul that year, with a campaign that included the execution of the official Emperor, Gratian. In 387, Magnus Maximus marched into Italy, intent on strengthening his position, but he was defeated in 388 by Theodosius I, a rival Emperor, and killed.

At the start of the fifth century, the Romans withdraw large numbers of troops from Britain, moving them to defend other parts of the Empire, which were being attacked by Goths and Vandals. In 407 the Roman authority in Britain proclaimed one of their generals as Constantine III, a rebel Emperor. Constantine III subsequently focussed on military campaigning in Gaul, and this led to the Britons expelling Roman officials in 409. With Rome struggling to counter invasions, the Empire did not seek to restore control of Britannia after this point. It appears that some forts situated along Hadrian's Wall were occupied by Britons, across the next few decades, before the structure was abandoned, and fell into disrepair. Thereafter material from the wall was recycled in other construction, including building work at Jarrow Priory, in the eighth century. The surviving parts of the wall, managed by the National Trust, have been a World Heritage Site since 1987.

3 Camelot

Rome was conquered by a Barbarian invasion in 476, and collapse of the Western Empire represents a major dividing line in European history. Antiquity ended, giving way to the Middle Ages – also called the Medieval period. In Britain, it had been common to refer to the post-Roman era, from 409, as the Dark Ages, due to an apparent lack of literacy. It is now realised that, in the next few centuries, our society developed in learning and organisation. Departure of the Romans, from what is now England and Wales, was followed by regular invasions of Picts and Scots. In about 425, Vortigern, a native of Wales, appears to have been recognised as high king of Britain. He had married Severa, daughter of Magnus Maximus, the rebel Roman Emperor. Vortigern hired Saxon mercenaries, to assist in the defence of his homeland. Relations between the Britons and Saxons soon became strained, and the latter started to make conquests here, as did the Angles and Jutes. The Saxons, Angles, and Jutes were three distinct groups within Germany, but have merged in the British national consciousness, becoming known as the Anglo-Saxons. At that point in our history, the term English is synonymous with the Anglo-Saxon invaders from Germany, pitched against the British, rather than native inhabitants of the territory that became England.

The earliest leader of the Picts for whom solid historic evidence exists is Drust Mac Erp, whose reign may have stretched from 424 to 453. During this period, Cunedda, a native of Manaw Gododdin, a British kingdom in what is now south east Scotland, fought as an ally of Vortigern. Relocating to the north of Wales, Cunedda defeated raiders from Ireland, and founded the kingdom of Gwynedd. He married Gwawl, daughter of Coel Hen, a shadowy British monarch to whom much legend has been attached. The suggestion that the nursery rhyme *Old King Cole*, first recorded in 1708, is based on Coel Hen is almost certainly erroneous. The idea that Coel gave his name to the town of Colchester is equally unlikely. Cunedda was succeeded as king of Gwynedd by a son, Einion Yrth, and then a grandson, Cadwallon Lawhir ap Einion.

The Anglo-Saxon era was destined to last for six hundred years, and prove more significant in our national history than four centuries of Roman rule. The first new kingdom was Kent, established by Hengest, who supposedly arrived with his brother, Horsa, in 449, leading a group of warriors invited over from the continent by Vortigern. The neighbouring Sussex, land of the South Saxons, was founded by Aelle in 491. Tradition recalls that King Arthur led the Britons in their fight against the Saxons. In the twelfth century, the Matter of Britain developed, as a series of tales revolving around the life of Arthur and the national identity. The perennial attraction of Arthur, the colossus of legend, stimulates search for the historical reality, much of which is shrouded in obscurity. The life of Cerdic, founder of Wessex, also forms a central part of a mysterious time, when the recording of events was not an important concern in this land. Over the last century, historians have increased our understanding of that age, through interpretation of archaeology and the few surviving ancient texts. In recent decades, a variety of British kings have been identified as possibly the true Arthur, and Cerdic has emerged as a candidate.

The prime source for Cerdic's activity, the *Anglo-Saxon Chronicle*, only features short references, and the dates reported are not certain. Frank Stenton's *Anglo-Saxon England*, a brilliant 700 page survey of the period, was published in 1943, as part of *The Oxford History of England*. This series covered a period of exactly two thousand years, from the first Roman incursion in 55 BCE to the end of World War Two in 1945 CE, with 15 volumes initially appearing between 1934 and 1965 – followed by revisions through until 1986. Eighty years after Stenton's book appeared, much of the detail has been superseded by later works, but his panorama has not been equalled. Stenton reproduced the following entries in the *Chronicle* relating to the establishment of Wessex.

495 Two chiefs, Cerdic and his son Cynric, came to Britain with five ships in the place called Cerdicesora, and fought with the Britons the same day.

501 Port and his two sons Bieda and Maegla came to Britain with two ships in the place called Portesmutha, and killed a young British man, a very noble man.

508 Cerdic and Cynric killed a British king called Natanleod, and five thousand men with him. That land was afterwards called Natanleaga as far as Cerdicesford.

514 The West Saxons, Stuf and Wihtgar, came to Britain with three ships in the place called Cerdicesora, and fought with the Britons and drove them into flight.

519 Cerdic and Cynric took the kingdom, and in the same year they fought with the Britons where it is now called Cerdicesford.

527 Cerdic and Cynric fought with the Britons in the place called Cerdicesleaga.

530 Cerdic and Cynric took the Isle of Wight, and killed a few men in the place called Wihtgaraesbyrg.

534 Cerdic died, and his son Cynric ruled for twenty-six years, and they gave the Isle of Wight to their nephews Stuf and Wihtgar.

Stenton succeeds in untangling some of the confusion, and overlap, inherent in these entries, which appeared in the *Anglo-Saxon Chronicle* about four centuries after the events began. Stenton argues that the quarter of a century of warfare leading to Cerdic establishing the kingdom of Wessex, suggested by the *Chronicle*, is the result of duplication.

Later scholars have shown that repetition in this part of the *Chronicle* occurs at 19 year intervals, with the annals having originally been written in tables used to calculate the dates for Easter – which recur in 19 year cycles. The entry for 527 is very similar to that of 508, and the entry for 514 may be a repeat of 495, but with the names of the invaders changed. Stenton mentions an entry inserted in the *Chronicle* when it was translated from English into Latin, by Ealdorman Ethelweard – a great grandson of King Ethelred of Wessex – late in the tenth century. This restored an annal stating that Cerdic conquered Wessex in the year 500. Stenton points out that a list of monarchs, prefixed to one manuscript of the *Chronicle*, records that Cerdic arrived in 494, and took control of Wessex around six years later. It therefore appears that the entry for 519 actually relates to Cerdic ruling Wessex in 500.

Cerdicesora, Cerdicesford, Cerdicesleaga, and Natanleaga have all been associated by historians with the area of Southampton and the southern part of the current Hampshire / Wiltshire border. Cerdicesora has been identified as Calshot, on the coast of Southampton Water. Cerdicesford is probably Charford in Hampshire, or possibly Downton in Wiltshire – the two villages are only a couple of miles apart. Natanleaga is apparently Netley Marsh, near Totton, a few miles west of Southampton. The Cerdicesleaga mentioned in the annal for 527 is probably the same place as either Cerdicesford or Natanleaga from the entry of 508. South west Hampshire and south east Wiltshire appears to have been the territory seized by Cerdic in 500, following which he, and his descendants, embarked upon creation of a larger Wessex.

Cerdic establishing Wessex just six years after his original invasion, without protracted war, is consistent, as Stenton demonstrates, with our earliest source for the period, *The Ruin of Britain* by Gildas. Stenton believed that this work was written in the years immediately prior to 547. Gildas recorded conflict between the Britons and Saxons, and mentioned that a British victory in the Battle of Badon Hill, which took place in the year of his birth, led to a peace maintained at the time of his writing, 44 years later. The evidence of Gildas, and the work of scholars in recent decades, places the Battle of Badon Hill within a few years of 500. *The History of the Britons*, written by Nennius, a Welshman, in around 828, describes Arthur leading the Britons as they won a series of twelve battles against the Saxons. The last, and greatest, victory was at Badon.

The entries for 495 and 534 in the *Chronicle* indicate that Cynric was the son of Cerdic. By contrast, genealogies of the Wessex monarchs, elsewhere in the *Chronicle*, consistently show Cynric to be the son of Creoda, who was the son of Cerdic. Stenton believed the latter of these alternatives to be correct. Cynric is said to have ruled Wessex from 534 to 560. Even if he was only a youth in 495, Cynric would probably have been aged over 80 by the time of his death, which appears unlikely. It appears that the annalists, recording events that were already part of the distant past, simply confused two men, and that it was Creoda, rather than Cynric, who joined the invasion of 495. The *Chronicle* places Cerdic's death in 534 but, if the 19 year dating error applies, the event occurred around 515. The *Chronicle* list of monarchs, which stated Cerdic took control of Wessex "within about six years" of his arrival in 494, added that he held the kingdom for 16 years. This appears to demonstrate that Cerdic ruled Wessex from 500 to 516, followed by Creoda, from 516 until 534, and then Cynric.

Alfred the Great was believed to be descended, via his mother Osburg, from Stuf and Wihtgar. This descent is mentioned in *The Life of King Alfred*, written by his contemporary, Bishop Asser. Stenton records that Stuf and Wihtgar were Jutes, and contends that they may have been the sons of a sister of Cerdic, and a Jutish man. Stenton writes "tradition is unanimous" that Cerdic was a Saxon, but suggests the name is British, probably being a version of the Welsh Ceretic. Stenton floated the possibility that Cerdic was the son of a Saxon father, and British mother. Modern scholars generally do not agree with the detail of Stenton's two speculations of inter-tribal marriage, but his indications were an important step towards enlightenment. Wessex did not assume that name, and identity as the land of the West Saxons, until the eighth century. Prior to that it was known as the land of the Gewisse. This name appears to have meant confederates, suggesting that the people who founded the territory were a combination of several tribes.

King Alfred was the twelve times great grandson of Cerdic. The *Chronicle* states that Cerdic was the son of a man named Elesa, who was the son of Gewis. The last of these names was an invention of Wessex genealogists, seeking a reason for their territory having been named Gewisse. The pedigree shows the supposed Gewis to be the great grandson of Woden, a Germanic God. Anglo-Saxon mythology in turn merged with the genealogies set out in the Bible, giving Cerdic a descent from Noah. A few generations earlier, the genealogy reaches Adam, the Biblical founder of the human race.

History and science have exploded the myth of Adam and Eve, and therefore the ultimate aim of the pedigree constructed for the Wessex monarchs, via Cerdic. In view of this, the ultimate achievement in British genealogy would be proof of descent from Beli Mawr, our first historical figure. Many people are able to claim such ancestry, via descent from early Welsh monarchs. These include Charles III, whose line has been traced through the Tudor ancestors of Henry VII. The discipline of research suggests it is unlikely that all the links in Welsh genealogies, written during the Medieval era, back to Beli Mawr, are correct. There is, however, the possibility of a complete lineage, across more than two thousand years of our history. The early generations include Bran the Blessed, a great grandson of Beli Mawr, supposedly marrying Anna, daughter of Joseph of Arimathea, the man reputed to have brought the Holy Grail to Britain – shortly after the death of Jesus Christ. This is story-telling in the grand manner.

The *Anglo-Saxon Chronicle* lacks any specific mention of King Arthur. One of the most prolific, and influential, writers about the man was Geoffrey Ashe. The best summary of his theory is *The Discovery of King Arthur* – published in 1985, with a revised edition following in 2003. Ashe argues that the basis for Arthur is the life of Riothamus, a British king who fought with the Romans, against the Goths, in Gaul, around 470. Ashe speculates that Cerdic may have been the son of Arthur. Advice from Ashe led to Arthur's court being located in Somerset, in the 1967 film *Camelot*, as a map of Britain appears on screen. The hill fort of South Cadbury, near the village of Queen Camel, in Somerset, was being excavated, due to belief it was the relevant site. This was led by the Camelot Research Committee, with promising results summarised in *The Quest for Arthur's Britain*, edited by Ashe, published in 1968. The earliest surviving references to Camelot in Arthurian literature do not appear until the twelfth century, but the ideal has become a central feature of the romances. Besides the link to Queen Camel, various other sources for the name Camelot have been suggested, including it being a corruption of Camlann, site of the battle at which Arthur was mortally wounded.

Northern England was colonised by Angles, who started to arrive around the year 500, and went on to rule two regions, Bernicia and Deira. These merged in an uneasy alliance, as the kingdom of Northumbria, at the start of the seventh century, but conflicts between the two groups meant that several times over the next few generations there were rival kings. Further north, establishment of the nation we know as Scotland was a gradual process, stretching across several centuries, and a few changes of name. At the end of the fifth century, the Scots set up a territory called Dal Riata, based around the area of Argyll, in western Scotland. Their leader, Fergus the Great, is recorded to have died in 501.

The East Saxons founded a territory in the mid-sixth century, based around the current-day Essex, but also including London, and some of the surrounding area to the north. At around this time, the East Angles established themselves in the area we still know as East Anglia. A separate group of Angles formed Mercia, in what is now the English midlands, with their first king being Creoda, who died in 593. Mercia included a number of sub-kingdoms – Hwicce, Lindsey, and Magonsaete – which were gradually subsumed, as Mercia became the strongest of the Anglo-Saxon territories. By the end of the sixth century, the only significant part of England left in the control of native Britons was Dumnonia, based around Cornwall and Devon. The kings of Dumnonia had close links with their fellow Britons in Wales, and some of them also ruled Brittany, in France. This stemmed from Brittany having been established by Celts, from south west Britain, in the fifth century.

The Celtic inhabitants of Britain displayed Pagan beliefs, and these were shared by the Anglo-Saxons, who worshipped Woden, rather than a Christian God. The roots of British Christianity, however, survived and subsequently flourished. Growth of the religion in Wales was supported by Maelgwn, king of Gwynedd, who died in 547. Maelgwn was a son of Cadwallon Lawhir ap Einion, his predecessor as ruler of Gwynedd, and therefore a great grandson of Cunedda. Maelgwn appears to have been recognised as pre-eminent among the various Welsh monarchs at the time. Saint David, the patron saint of Wales, founded a monastery in Pembrokeshire, at the site which is now the city of St David's. David died on March 1, possibly in the year 589. Nowadays St David's Day is marked by the people of Wales on March 1 each year, with this also being the first day of meteorological Spring in Britain (there is no official start of Spring). David Lloyd George, a Welshman who was Liberal Prime Minister of Britain from 1916 to 1922, popularised the wearing of daffodils on St David's Day. The daffodil, a beautiful signal of the start of Spring, is the national flower of contemporary Wales.

In 563 Saint Columba, an Irish monk, arrived on Iona, an island that was then part of Dal Riata, and is now one of the Hebrides. Columba set about converting people in Scotland to Christianity. He was also present, when visiting the Picts, at the earliest recorded sighting of the Loch Ness Monster. This is set out in the *Life of St. Columba* – venerated as "the blessed man" – written at the end of the seventh century by Saint Adomnan. Columba was at the River Ness, which flows from the loch:

He saw some of the inhabitants burying an unfortunate man who, according to the account of those who were burying him, was a short time before seized, as he was swimming, and bitten most severely by a monster that lived in the water. His wretched body was, though too late, taken out with a hook, by those who came to his assistance in a boat.

A companion of Columba, named Lugne Mocu-Min, started to swim across the river, to collect a moored fishing boat. Adomnan records that:

The monster, which so far from being satiated, was only roused for more prey, was lying at the bottom of the stream, and when it felt the water disturbed above by the man swimming, suddenly rushed out, and, giving an awful roar, darted after him, with its mouth wide open, as the man swam in the middle of the stream. Then the blessed man observing this, raised his holy hand, while all the rest, brethren as well as strangers, were stupefied with terror and, invoking the name of God, formed the saving sign of the cross in the air, and commanded the ferocious monster, saying "Thou shalt go no further, nor touch the man, go back with all speed". Then at the voice of the saint, the monster was terrified, and fled more quickly than if it had been pulled back with ropes.

The modern cult of the monster stems from a series of alleged sightings, beginning in 1933. Scientific surveys of the Loch have failed to provide confirmation, while there are many theories to explain the phenomenon. At the start of 2006, several newspapers reported an amusing revelation, enabled by the Freedom of Information Act. In 1979, shortly after the election of Margaret Thatcher's Conservative government, ministers and civil servants considered a search for the monster, using dolphins with underwater cameras attached to them. It was hoped that proof, if it could be found, of the existence of Nessie would boost tourism.

Saint Columba died, on Iona, in 597, following which Christian work was continued by other missionaries, but Scotland remained divided between various tribes, with protracted conflicts. The year 597 also saw the arrival, in Kent, of Augustine, a Roman monk sent by Pope Gregory I. Augustine converted King Ethelbert of Kent, and established himself as the first Archbishop of Canterbury. The role survived the English break from the Roman Catholic Church, led by Henry VIII in the sixteenth century. The Archbishop of Canterbury remains the leading religious figure in the Church of England – subordinate to the British monarch, who is Supreme Governor of the church.

The agreement, in about 600, of a law code for Kent, put forward by King Ethelbert, is the earliest recorded action of a Witenagemot. The name, meaning "meeting of wise men", is often shortened to Witan. It was a loose assembly of nobles and churchmen, summoned when they were required to advise the monarch in various Anglo-Saxon territories. The origin of the Witan has been found in similar bodies in Germany, known as folkmoots. The Witan nominally had a role in electing monarchs, who could be selected from among the men of royal blood, who were known as Atheling, a title which meant throne-worthy. In practice, the Witan was normally only used to ratify succession of the male heir of a deceased king. Theoretically a Witan could depose a monarch, but there are only two recorded instances – the departing kings being Sigeberht of Wessex in 757, and Alhred of Northumbria in 774. Following the Norman Conquest, the Witan was abolished, and replaced by a royal council, the Curia Regis. The latter was in turn superseded by the establishment of the English Parliament, in the thirteenth century. A Witan sometimes included women members, something which was not replicated in the United Kingdom Parliaments until the twentieth century.

The present-day county system of local government administration has its origins in the Anglo-Saxon period. The *Chronicle* entry for the year 755 mentions Hamtunscir, this being the area of Wessex around the town of Hamtun. These names would develop into Hampshire and Southampton respectively. The shire system subsequently expanded to the rest of Wessex, and in the tenth century stretched across most of England. Each shire was overseen by an official, appointed by the monarchy, known as a Shire Reeve, a title which later became Sheriff. The role of Sheriff has evolved over the centuries, and counties in contemporary England and Wales have a High Sheriff, fulfilling a largely ceremonial role.

During the course of the seventh and eighth centuries, rulers of the Anglo-Saxon kingdoms gradually adopted Christianity, and the English church gained in strength. A group of bishoprics were established, following on from Canterbury, and a man named Wine (an Anglo-Saxon word meaning "friend") became the first Bishop of Winchester in 660. Wine moved to become Bishop of London in 666 – the devil is in the detail. Daniel, Bishop of Winchester from about 705 until 744, provided information which helped the Venerable Bede write the *Ecclesiastical History of the English People*, completed around 731. Bede's work contains the earliest surviving native reference to the ancient name for this land, as he wrote "Britain, an island in the ocean, formerly called Albion, is situated between the north and west, facing, though at a considerable distance, the coasts of Germany, France, and Spain, which form the greatest part of Europe".

Bede records the names of seven kings, who held "Imperium", a term which appears to mean the overlordship of their contemporaries as Anglo-Saxon monarchs. These men, with the dates they ruled individual territories, are:

> Aelle of Sussex, 491-circa 516
> Ceawlin of Wessex, 560-592
> Ethelbert of Kent, circa 589-616
> Redwald of East Anglia, circa 599-circa 625
> Edwin of Northumbria, 616-633
> Oswald of Northumbria, 634-642
> Oswy of Northumbria, 642-670

A continuous run of "Imperium" can be plotted, between the rise of Ceawlin of Wessex, in the mid-sixth century, and the reign of Oswy of Northumbria, in the mid-seventh century. Nevertheless the position seems to have been retrospectively bestowed upon the men who held it, as individual recipients did not assert the title during their lifetimes.

Perhaps the most recognisable symbol of Anglo-Saxon England is the Sutton Hoo helmet. This was found in a ship burial, excavated at Sutton Hoo, in Suffolk, in 1939, shortly before the start of World War Two. Edith Pretty, the woman who commissioned the search on her land, donated the finds to the nation. The artefacts, including the broken remains of the helmet, were stored in a tunnel in the London Underground rail network, for the duration of the war. The helmet was reconstructed in the months after hostilities ended, and has remained on display at the British Museum since then. The identity of the man buried with the helmet is uncertain, but the most likely candidate is Redwald, king of East Anglia, and the fourth monarch listed by Bede.

The next three holders of "Imperium" were from Northumbria, a kingdom which gained wide influence across northern England, Wales, and Scotland. Cadwallon ap Cadfan, who became king of Gwynedd in about 625, was forced to defend his territory against Edwin, king of Northumbria, who moved westwards, conquering both Anglesey and the Isle of Man. Cadwallon arranged an alliance with Penda, king of Mercia, whereupon their combined forces defeated, and killed, Edwin at the Battle of Hatfield Chase (near Doncaster, now in South Yorkshire), during 633. Cadwallon ruled much of Northumbria, until he in turn was killed the following year, at the Battle of Heavenfield (fought near the current town of Chollerford, in Northumberland), by Oswald, who became the new ruler of Northumbria. The Northumbrians annexed much of south east Scotland in the seventh century, including Eidyn – the region of the current Edinburgh – in 638.

Oswald was killed by Penda's Mercian army in 642, at the Battle of Maserfield (the probable location being Oswestry, in Shropshire). A sister of Penda – her name is now unknown – married Cenwalh, who became king of Wessex in about 643. Cenwalh soon repudiated his Mercian wife, and married Seaxburgh, whose origin is not recorded. This action provoked Penda to invade Wessex, and depose Cenwahl, who took refuge with Anna, king of East Anglia – a nephew of Redwald. Cenwalh regained his position as monarch of Wessex, after about three years in exile. Following the death of Cenwalh, in 672, Seaxburgh took power, and ruled Wessex for a year or two, appearing to have been the only queen regnant in any Anglo-Saxon territory. Penda of Mercia was killed in 665, at the Battle of Winwaed (probably near Leeds, West Yorkshire), against Oswy, king of Northumberland, who had succeeded his brother, Oswald. Oswy chaired the Synod of Whitby, held in 664, which decided that the date of Easter would be calculated in line with the practice of the Roman Catholic Church, as opposed to an alternative that had been favoured by Saint Columba. The settlement of this Easter question, for Northumbria, was subsequently adhered to across England.

After the death of Oswy, the Picts, led by Brude Mac Bili (reigned 672-693), regained freedom from the Northumbrians, winning the Battle of Nechtansmere in 685. Cadwaladr, a son of Cadwallon, who ruled Gwynedd from about 655 until 682, was the last man described as a king of Britain by Geoffrey of Monmouth. Cadwaladr is traditionally supposed to have introduced the red dragon as an emblem of Wales. The red dragon appears on the modern Welsh flag, set against a green and white background – the latter being colours associated with the Tudor dynasty.

Mercia displaced Northumbria as the strongest Anglo-Saxon kingdom, in the eighth century. Aethelbald, ruler of Mercia from 716 to 757, gained effective control of London – previously part of the kingdom of the East Saxons. A charter of 736 describes Aethelbald as "rex Britanniae", Latin equivalent of "king of Britain". He claimed, in a 746 charter, to be king of the "gens Anglorum" (the Angle people), and this led to Aethelbald's subjects referring to themselves as the Aenglisc, which in turn developed into the word English. Aethelbald was murdered by his bodyguards, following which the next monarch, Beornred, was deposed by Offa, with both events happening in 757.

Offa ruled Mercia until 796, and built Offa's Dyke, an earthwork stretching for about 150 miles, from the River Dee to the River Severn, marking the frontier between Mercia and Wales. Much of the dyke survives into the present day, being the most impressive physical remnant of Anglo-Saxon England. The work appears to have commenced in the late 780s, by which time the monarchs of the neighbouring Welsh territories had probably accepted Offa's primacy within both England and Wales, following Mercian military campaigns. Both Aethelbald and Offa had become more powerful than most of Bede's "Imperium" monarchs, several of whom lacked significant influence outside their local territory.

Offa introduced the silver penny as the basic unit of English coinage, importing an idea from Francia, as France was then known. In 780 Francia moved from a currency that featured both gold and silver coinage to a new system, based exclusively on silver. Francia divided a pound weight of silver into 240 deniers, their equivalent of a penny. This method of division was also to be used in Britain, with 240 pennies in a pound (made up of 20 shillings, with 12 pence in each). The pounds, shillings and pence system was replaced by decimalisation in 1971, when a pound was divided into one hundred new pence (the "new" part of the name would be dropped in 1982). A silver penny, with the name of a monarch on one side, and that of the moneyer who minted it on the reverse, was the basis of English currency from the time of Offa through to Henry III (reigned 1216-1272).

During Offa's lifetime, Britain experienced a severe new threat. The first Norwegian Viking attack appears to have taken place in 789, on the coast of Dorset, in Wessex. This was followed by desolation of the monastery at Lindisfarne, in 793. Lindisfarne was part of Northumbria, which bore much of the brunt of the invasions, from across the North Sea, over the next few decades. Further north, the eighth century had seen continuation of a struggle for dominance between the Picts and Scots. Angus I, king of the Picts from 729 to 761, also ruled the Dal Riata Scots between 736 and 750, making himself the strongest monarch up to that point in Scotland, but was deposed in Dal Riata by Aed the Fair, who ruled until 778. Internal strife was complicated by the arrival of the Vikings, who raided Iona in 795. This began a campaign that brought conquest of the Hebrides, and also the Isle of Man. Vikings set up what is known as the Kingdom of the Isles in these territories, during the ninth century, and were destined to hold parts of it through to the thirteenth century. The Isle of Man regained independence in 1266, becoming part of Scotland. Ownership of the island subsequently transferred to the crown of England, and then Britain. The Isle of Man is now a self-governing Crown Dependency, a status shared with both Guernsey and Jersey. The Channel Islands are not part of the United Kingdom, but Charles III is head of state, and informally known as the Duke of Normandy.

4 Anglo-Saxon Chronicle

The British monarchy is a perennial focus of public attention. Alongside discussion of contemporary events in the royal family, there is much talk about the traditions of the monarchy. Who was the first king of England? Many books seem to suggest it was William the Conqueror, with the view that the Norman Conquest of 1066 was so significant that the preceding millennium, and more, of English history can be ignored. At the other extreme, it is possible to consider the 106 rulers recorded in the *History of the Kings of Britain* by Geoffrey of Monmouth, written about 1136, as our original monarchs. Geoffrey's figureheads apparently stretch from about 800 BCE through to the late seventh century CE, but much of his narrative is myth, with little basis in fact.

The conventional approach sees the origin of the English, and later British, monarchy in the House of Wessex. This view makes Egbert of Wessex the first king of England, and accords that role to each of his successors in Wessex, through to the undisputed kings of England, who emerged a century later. Several Wessex monarchs could not claim anything near the dominance Egbert enjoyed, having to contend with rival territories and rulers. Retrospective recognition of Egbert as the first king of England is an act of historical convenience.

Relatively sparse information is available about the activities of Egbert. His birth is not recorded, but the consensus among historians suggests this happened in the late 760s. He was claimed to be a ten times great grandson of Cerdic, founder of Wessex, and the son of Eahlmund, who had two short spells as king of Kent – the approximate dates being from 762 to 764, and then 784 to 785. Both of Eahlmund's reigns ended with deposition at the hands of Offa, king of Mercia, and on the second occasion Eahlmund was probably killed. The earliest known incident in Egbert's life occurred in 786 when he contested for the throne of Wessex, following the death of King Cynewulf. This bid for power failed, as Egbert's rival Beorhtric was able to establish himself as king, with support from Offa. In 789 Beorhtric strengthened his alliance with Mercia, by marrying Eadburh, a daughter of Offa. At the same time, Offa and Beorhtric forced Egbert into exile.

The young Egbert spent about a decade overseas, including a spell of three years with Charlemagne, king of the Franks, who established an empire that stretched across much of Europe. Egbert may have been offered refuge with Charlemagne due to traditional connections between Kent and Francia. Offa of Mercia had enjoyed good relations with Charlemagne, until a rift opened in 789. Charlemagne suggested that his son Charles marry one of Offa's daughters. Offa made agreement subject to his son, Ecgfrith, marrying Bertha, a daughter of Charlemagne. Offa's wish, via the proposed double marriage, to be recognised as an equal of Charlemagne annoyed the latter. Charlemagne signified his displeasure by temporarily blocking trade between England and Francia. In the longer term, and more significantly, Charlemagne's friendship towards Offa and Mercia waned, and Egbert was to be a resulting beneficiary. Egbert found a wife at the Carolingian court, marrying Redburga, who appears to have been a sister, niece, or sister-in-law of Charlemagne.

Beorhtric ruled Wessex as a dependency of Mercia. His actions were dominated by Eadburh, who was jealous of the friendships developed by Beorhtric, and apparently used poison to murder several of his closest confidants. This eventually backfired upon Eadburh, as in 802 she accidentally killed Beorhtric, when he consumed a poisoned drink intended for one of his friends. The people of Wessex, who detested Eadburh, subsequently recalled her in a preposterous legend, which is worth repeating for its originality. Eadburh, it was claimed, fled to Francia after killing Beorhtric, and sought refuge with Charlemagne. The emperor – a man known for having multiple wives and concubines – offered Eadburh marriage to either himself or one of his sons, and she chose the latter. Offended by this decision, Charlemagne banished Eadburh from his court, and she lived the remainder of her life as a beggar in Francia.

Returning to verifiable fact, Egbert gained the throne of Wessex upon the death of Beorhtric. At that time the territory consisted of the equivalent of modern-day Hampshire, Wiltshire, Dorset, Somerset, and Devon. In view of Egbert's position as the grandfather of King Alfred, the man who oversaw the initial work on the *Anglo-Saxon Chronicle*, that history has surprisingly little material on Egbert. The first reference occurs in the annal for 802, recording a victory for "the men of Wiltshire" over the Wiccians, from Mercia. Kempsford, the scene of the battle, is now situated in Gloucestershire, a few miles north of the border with Wiltshire. Egbert began the enlargement of Wessex in 815, with a campaign that effectively annexed Cornwall.

In 825 Egbert returned to Cornwall, and defeated rebels in a battle at Camelford. The Mercians, led by King Beornwulf, invaded the main part of Wessex, hoping to take advantage of Egbert's absence in the west country. Egbert returned to his core territory, and led the army of Wessex to victory over the Mercians at Ellendun (now Ellendune, near Wroughton) in Wiltshire. Egbert sent a large detachment of the Wessex army, led by his son Ethelwulf, in search of territorial gain. Ethelwulf rapidly conquered the territory which is now Surrey, Sussex, Kent, and Essex, all of which had been under Mercian control. The capture of Kent – and expulsion of the puppet monarch, Baldred – was a contrast to Eahlmund, the father of Egbert, having twice been deprived of this territory by Offa. The events of 825 are described at length in the *Anglo-Saxon Chronicle*, which reports that "The king of the East Angles, and the people, besought King Egbert to give them peace and protection against the terror of the Mercians". In 826 Beornwulf of Mercia invaded East Anglia, but was killed by the forces of the latter territory. Beornwulf was succeeded by King Ludeca, who invaded East Anglia in 827, attempting to avenge the death of his predecessor. Lightning struck twice, as Ludeca was slain by the East Angles.

The advance of Wessex culminated in 829, as Egbert conquered Mercia, deposing its monarch, Wiglaf. The Wessex army continued to march northwards, intent upon annexation of Northumbria. Forestalling this threat, King Eanred of Northumbria met the invaders at Dore (near Sheffield), and offered submission to Egbert. Eanred was one of the strongest monarchs of Northumbria – during a reign that stretched from 811 to 843 – but did not feel equal to a war at this point. The *Chronicle* entry for 829 states that Egbert was now the eighth Bretwalda, an Anglo-Saxon word meaning "ruler of Britain". The preceding Bretwaldas are then listed, being the seven monarchs to whom Bede gave the title "Imperium". The last of these, Oswy of Northumbria, had died over a century and a half earlier, back in 670.

In 830 the Mercians carried out a successful rebellion against Wessex, and restored Wiglaf to their throne. On the other hand, Egbert made an incursion into Wales during that year, forcing the submission of Cyngen ap Cadell, the king of Powys. Egbert remained effective overlord of England, and part of Wales, for the remainder of his life. Despite this, the widest title Egbert is recorded to have used was "King of the West Saxons and Kentishmen", while in 829 Egbert proclaimed himself "King of Mercia".

Egbert spent the final years of his reign on the defensive, with the need to meet attacks by Danish Vikings. The *Anglo-Saxon Chronicle* entry for 835 records "This year heathen men overran the Isle of Sheppey". The term "heathen men" was one of the variety of ways in which the annalists described the Vikings. The attack on Sheppey, in Kent, was followed in the next year by another Danish landing in Wessex. The *Chronicle* annal for 836 states that Egbert was defeated in a battle against Danish "pirates". The location of this clash was possibly Charmouth, in Dorset. The Danes, encouraged by their initial success, entered into an unholy alliance with the Cornish, who had hopes of regaining their independence from Wessex. In 838 news of a Danish invasion in the west country, and the growing rebellion of the Cornish, prompted Egbert to lead his army to the area. The forces of Wessex defeated a combined Cornish and Danish army, as they clashed at Hengeston (now Hingston Down, near

Callington) in Cornwall. The battle effectively ended Cornish attempts at separatism. Egbert died in 839, aged about 70.

Theorists of the British monarchy proudly assert that a continuous line of descent is traceable from Egbert, in the ninth century, to Charles III, in the present day. This supposedly gives British royalty a historic tradition, and stability, lacking in other monarchies. In practice, only the English version that can be traced back to 829. The British monarchy stems from the accidental unification of the crowns of England and Scotland, in the person of James I, in 1603, and legal ratification of the combined state in 1707. The present king can trace direct descent from Egbert – his thirty seven times great grandfather – but the intervening period has seen breaks in the succession. Six kings who were not descended from Egbert reigned during the eleventh century. These were Swein, Cnut, Harold Harefoot, and Harthacnut (each from the Danish royal family), followed by Harold Godwinson (an English nobleman), and William the Conqueror (from Normandy). There was a greater upheaval six centuries later, as England experienced a spell as a republic between 1649 and 1660.

The English monarchy has fallen into the hands of a series of dynasties, with only a minority of them being English. The rule of the Normans. The Normans were followed by fellow-Frenchmen, the Plantagenets. The Houses of Lancaster and York, who fought against each other in the Wars of the Roses, were mostly of English birth, but also sub-dynasties of the Plantagenets. Henry V, the greatest of the Lancastrians, was born in Wales, and Edward IV, the first of the Yorkists, was born in Normandy. The Plantagenets were followed by the Tudors, from Wales, and the Stuarts, from Scotland. The crown then passed to the Hanoverians, who were German. They in turn were succeeded by the present dynasty, which combines English birth with German ancestry. The royal family's German surname, Saxe-Coburg-Gotha – the German principality of Albert, the husband of Queen Victoria – was changed to Windsor, by patriotic sleight of hand, during World War One. The decision was made in 1917 by George V (reigned 1910-1936), with the idea for the new surname coming from discovery that Edward III had been known as "Edward of Windsor", due to his birth in Windsor Castle, during 1312.

Egbert's effective position as the original English monarch precludes that role being assigned to any of the romantic figures who preceded him. Geoffrey of Monmouth's *History of the Kings of Britain* features such monarchs as Brutus, Lear, Queen Cordelia, Beli Mawr (whom Geoffrey refers to as Heli), Llud, Caswallon, Cymbeline (the name given by Geoffrey, and William Shakespeare, to a king who was actually named Cunobelin), Lucius, Coel Hen, Vortigern, and Arthur. By contrast,

Geoffrey does not mention Boudicca, who challenged the Roman invaders in the first century. Retrospective recognition of Egbert as Bretwalda, in the *Anglo-Saxon Chronicle*, several decades after his death, was apparently motivated by a wish to link Alfred, as reigning monarch of Wessex, to a grandfather who was a dominant English king. The material on Egbert in the *Chronicle* can be considered the infant English monarchy's view of its establishment. The present day Official Website of the British Royal Family does not offer a specific pronouncement on who was the first king of England. Biographical sketches of English monarchs start with Offa of Mercia, who is noted as "the first ruler to be called 'king of the English'". The website's curious piece on Egbert merely states:

As King of Wessex, after the decline of Mercian power under Offa, Egbert inherited the mantle of 'bretwalda' – an Anglo-Saxon term meaning a ruler with overall superiority to other rulers He came to power in 802 and died in 839, but little else is known about his reign.

The contemporary compilers of the royal website have overlooked the material collected by their predecessors, when work commenced on the *Anglo-Saxon Chronicle*.

Egbert's historic importance has been overshadowed by the cultural fame of an advisor, Swithin. The latter was born around the year 800, near Winchester, and acted as tutor to Ethelwulf, a son of Egbert. As king of Wessex. Ethelwulf appointed Swithin as Bishop of Winchester, in 852. Besides tending to the spiritual needs of people in Winchester, the bishop organised building of a wall – to defend the city against Viking raids – and a bridge across the River Itchen. A mythical tale has been told of Swithin seeing a woman, who was crossing the bridge to sell eggs at a market, being jostled by men, with the result that the eggs were broken. The sympathetic bishop is supposed to have promptly mended the woman's eggs, whereupon she proceeded to the market as planned. Swithin died on July 2 862, and was buried outside Winchester Cathedral, in accordance with his wish that "the sweet rain from heaven may fall upon my grave".

The decades following Swithin's death saw the development of a cult around his remains, to which miracles were attributed. Ethelwold, Bishop of Winchester, appointed in 963, oversaw a rebuilding of the cathedral. Ethelwold arranged for Swithin's body to be re-buried inside the cathedral, and the movement of the remains, on July 15 971, was followed by a spectacular storm. The storm was later reputed to be the start of 40 days of rain, which led to a legend. Forty days was doubtless an exaggeration of this period of rain, but is significant as an attempt to assert an English equivalent of the Biblical flood, from which Noah and his family, along with representatives of the animal kingdom, escaped in the Ark. The Anglo-Saxon monarchy was keen to express connections with the Biblical roots of Christianity and humanity, with the official genealogy of the Wessex kings stretching back to Adam. One of these monarchs' supposed ancestors was Seth – a son of Noah – of whom the *Anglo-Saxon Chronicle* stated that "he was born in Noah's Ark". Swithin appears once in the *Chronicle*, with his death mistakenly placed in the year 861.

The writings of scholars transformed Swithin from a man of merely Wessex interest into a national figure. *Lives of the Saints*, by Aelfric "the Grammarian", recorded pilgrimages to Winchester Cathedral, in memory of Swithin, during the latter part of the tenth century. "Within ten days", Aelfric wrote, "two hundred men were healed, and so many within twelve months that no man could count them. The burial ground lay filled with crippled folk so that one could not easily visit the cathedral".

Following the Norman Conquest, the new rulers of England rebuilt Winchester Cathedral, with work on the current structure starting in 1079. Saint Swithin's Shrine was moved, during 1093, to the new Cathedral from the Old Minster, as the Anglo-Saxon building is known, following which the original construction was demolished. Swithin was venerated as the patron saint of Winchester Cathedral, and the shrine remained a focal point for pilgrims. In the present day, we can consider the rather obscure events of Swithin's life, and feel confident that his surprisingly large reputation will continue to influence our folklore, in view of the British obsession with the weather.

Britain had its wettest ever (recorded) year in 2000, with a severe concentration of rain in the Autumn. Day after day, and night after night, it rained and rained. The relentless rain led to floods on a scale unparalleled in recent decades. Many towns and villages were submerged as swollen rivers burst their banks, and people navigating along roads by boat rescued others who were stranded by the water. Britain suddenly had its equivalents of Noah's Ark. It also appeared that the legend of Saint Swithin had come true, albeit with the 40 days of rain commencing in September, instead of on July 15. Attention is normally focussed on the idea that if it rains on Saint Swithin's Day it will rain for each of the next 40 days. This has always seemed improbable, given that the date falls in the middle of Summer. The flip side is that good weather on Saint Swithin's Day will continue for a period of 40 days. That seems fairly reasonable – or does it, in view of the unreliable nature of the British Summer?

Fast forward nearly seven years from the Autumn of 2000, and Britain experienced another prolonged spell of rain, and further flooding. The deluge of 2007, however, stretched across May, June, and July, as Spring was followed by Summer, and July 15 was one of the many dates on which it rained. Recollections of the legend of Saint Swithin's Day were combined with concerned debate, as the flooding caused the death of several people, and it appeared global warming was having a seriously adverse effect upon the British climate. Five years later, in 2012, Britain had its wettest Summer since 1912. The weather was also getting warmer, with 2014 having the highest temperature across the year since British records began in 1910. Several other years in the early part of the twenty first century were also warmer than average. The Summer of 2018 saw a prolonged heatwave, with the average temperature across the United Kingdom for the season equalling previous records, set in 1976, 2003, and 2006.

In the decades following the death of Egbert, contemporaries did not consider the Wessex monarchs to be kings of the whole nation. Ethelwulf (839-855) was followed as ruler of Wessex by four sons in succession, Ethelbald (855-860), Ethelbert (860-865), Ethelred (865-871), and Alfred (871-899). Egbert's family renewed their dynastic link with the Carolingians in an unusual way. In 856 Ethelwulf, who had abdicated as king of Wessex the previous year, married Judith, a great granddaughter of Charlemagne. This political alliance was a personal mismatch, as a man aged around 60 married a girl of about 13. Ethelwulf died in 858, whereupon his son Ethelbald promptly married Judith, a stepmother who appears to have been a decade younger than him. An outraged church annulled the incestuous marriage within a few months.

Judith was to have a further influence upon the English monarchy, through her third marriage, to Baldwin I, Count of Flanders. Their son, Baldwin II, married Elfrida, a daughter of King Alfred. Matilda of Flanders, a four times great granddaughter of Baldwin II and Elfrida, married the man who became William the Conqueror. It was to this lineage that three English kings, William II (1087-1100), Henry I (1100-1135), and Stephen (1135-1154), owed their descent from Egbert. All English monarchs subsequent to Stephen have also been descended from Egbert via Matilda of Scotland – a wife of Henry I – who was a great granddaughter of Edmund II, the latter of whom ruled England for a few months in 1016.

Egbert's successors in Wessex led the English fight against the Viking threat, co-ordinating efforts with the monarchs of other kingdoms at vital moments. Large parts of Northumbria and Mercia were conquered by the Vikings in the 860s and 870s. Thereafter King Alfred spent much of his reign embroiled in heroic defence of Wessex, which halted the momentum of the Vikings – he also burned some loaves, or cakes. With the invaders controlling much of the north and the midlands, the title "King of the English", which Alfred used on his coins, was a fair representation of his role as national leader.

The nickname Alfred the Great did not arrive until the sixteenth century, being coined following the English Reformation, as writers acclaimed Alfred as a defender of English independence. Alfred's remains were lost as an indirect result of that Reformation. His body was originally buried in Winchester, but subsequently moved to the nearby Hyde Abbey, which was largely demolished in 1539, during the Dissolution of the Monasteries. The graves of Alfred and his son, King Edward, were left intact, but also abandoned, and eventually destroyed in 1788, as a prison was built on the site of the abbey.

The prominent role of Wessex, in ninth century England, was mirrored by moves towards unification in Scotland. Angus II inherited the kingdoms of both the Picts and Scots in 820, and reigned until 834. Angus saw a vision of Saint Andrew (a disciple of Jesus Christ) on the eve of the Battle of Athelstaneford, fought in 832 against an invading force from Northumbria. Victory in the battle led to Angus promoting Andrew as a patron saint for Scotland, and he continues to be remembered on November 30 each year. Saint Andrew's Day did not, however, become a Bank Holiday until an Act of the Scottish Parliament was passed in 2007. Kenneth MacAlpin, a Scottish king, managed to conquer the lands of the Picts. Kenneth's rule is traditionally dated from 843, but he did not exert full authority until 848. Kenneth called his territory Alba, this being a Scottish Gaelic variant on the word Albion, originally used to describe the whole of Britain.

Kenneth was succeeded as monarch by his brother, Donald I (858-863) and then two sons, Constantine I (863-877) and Aed (877-878). Aed was a weak king, deposed by his cousin Giric (878-899), who was a son of Donald I. Giric in turn was deposed by a son of Constantine I, who ruled as Donald II (889-900). Donald II was the first monarch to be officially recognised as king of Alba, with the name Alba being used interchangeably with Scotland at that time. Donald II died in 900, the year after the death of Alfred the Great. More than eight hundred years after the people of what became England and Scotland separately defended their respective lands against the Romans, and following several changes of identity, two states had clearly been founded.

The inhabitants of Wales saw themselves as defenders of the traditional Britain, in the face of the spread of Anglo-Saxon power in England. People living in Wales called their territory Cymru, a name derived from the ancient British "combrogi", which meant "fellow-countrymen". This in turn led to Cambria emerging as a Latinised version of Cymru, used by people outside that land. The Anglo-Saxons used the word "walha" which meant "foreigner", and this later became the name Wales, as a way to distinguish that country from England. In the present day, Cymru remains the official native name of the relevant territory, within the United Kingdom. England annexed Wales in the sixteenth century but the local language, Cymraeg, survives and flourishes.

Hywel ap Rhodri Molywynog, the last king of Gwynedd to be descended in the male line from Cunedda, was succeeded in about 825 by a nephew, Merfyn the Freckled, who ruled until around 844. Rhodri Mawr (Rhodri the Great), who followed his father, Merfyn, as king of Gwynedd, made himself the master of most of Wales, expanding territory with a combination of conquest and inheritance – via his wife, Angharad ferch Meurig, a member of the royal family of Ceredigion. Rhodri successfully defended his land against invasions by the Vikings, but apparently died, in about 878, in a battle against Anglo-Saxons. Following Rhodri's death, the territory was divided among several sons, who in turn founded a series of dynasties, between whom power was to shift in Wales over the next few generations. Anarawd ap Rhodri, king of Gwynedd (circa 878-circa 916), formed an alliance with Alfred the Great, defending against Viking incursions. Anarawd's son, Idwal (circa 916-942), allied with Athelstan, the grandson of Alfred, but later clashed with the English, and was killed in battle.

Alfred was followed as king of Wessex by his son, Edward the Elder (899-924), much of whose reign was taken up with battles against the Vikings. Edward's son, Athelstan (924-939), was accepted as king of Mercia as well as Wessex. Athelstan, whose name meant noble stone, gained the submission of the Welsh kings, at Hereford, in 926. The following year, Constantine II of Scotland (900-943) – a cousin of his predecessor, Donald II – also paid homage to Athelstan, at Eamont Bridge, in Cumbria. Athelstan's coinage proclaimed him as "Rex Totius Britannie", meaning "King of all Britain". He was clearly the strongest English king to date, and from this point onwards all of the Wessex monarchs can reasonably be identified as the kings of England. Constantine II, who had spent much of his reign defending Scotland from Vikings, suddenly allied with Olaf Gothrithson, a Viking King of Dublin, during 934. Constantine and Olaf invaded England in 937, but were defeated by Athelstan, in the Battle of Brunanburh – the location of which is a mystery. Six years later, and after 43 years as king, Constantine II abdicated, and retired to a monastery, being succeeded by

Malcolm I (943-954), a son of Donald II. Hywel Dda (Hywel the Good), king of Deheubarth – one of the monarchs who accepted the overlordship of Athelstan – conquered Gwynedd during 942, making himself effective ruler of most of Wales until his death, in 950. Gwynedd then regained independence, being led by Idwal and Iago, sons of the previous monarch, Idwal. In 986, Gwynedd was again conquered, this time by Maredudd ab Owain, king of Deheubarth, who emulated his grandfather, Hywel Dda, in ruling most of Wales.

The first coronation of a man as king of all England did not occur until 144 years after Egbert supposedly became the Bretwalda. King Edgar (959-975) was crowned in 973, along with his queen, Elfrida of Devon, in a ceremony officiated by Dunstan, Archbishop of Canterbury, at Bath Abbey. Elements were to be repeated at the coronation of Charles III in 2023 – one thousand and fifty years later. Shortly after Edgar's coronation, several Welsh monarchs plus Kenneth II of Scotland (971-995) – who was a son of Malcolm I – paid homage to him, at Chester. Edgar's power within England was not, however, complete. From the time that Vikings first conquered Northumbria and Mercia, a century earlier, the Danish nobility maintained a degree of control in this region, known as the Danelaw.

Englalonde, the name by which the country was known in the latter part of the Anglo-Saxon period, gradually became a fairly unified nation, and several themes of importance emerged, including lasting features of government administration and law. The earlier ideals of a high king (pre-eminent among various tribal leaders), and Bretwalda (a leading figure among several developing kingdoms), developed into a national monarchy, in which a single king, drawn from an established ruling dynasty, was clearly head of state. The king was the ultimate source, and guardian, of a legal system. Systematic codification of English laws was led by King Edgar.

At the start of the second millennium, England was ruled by a man widely recalled as Ethelred "the Unready". This suggests that he was simply not prepared for the responsibilities required of a king, but the meaning is more subtle. The Ethelred was born around 968, being a son of King Edgar. When Edgar died, in 975, he was succeeded by his elder son, Edward, who was still a child. The government of England fell into the hands of the nobility, who were divided into factions. In 978 Edward was murdered by members of Ethelred's household, at Corfe, in Dorset. Ethelred, aged about nine, was proclaimed king by his supporters who, along with his mother, Elfrida of Devon, ruled the country for several years. In the present day, the stark ruins of Corfe Castle reflect its virtual destruction in 1646, following capture by Parliamentary forces in the

Civil War. The castle was built in the Norman period, and remains of an earlier Anglo-Saxon building have been found within the grounds – probably the home of Elfrida and Ethelred during his childhood. Ethelred was innocent of involvement in the murder, but the manner in which he became king was to undermine the new monarch's rule. Edward gained a reputation as the performer of miracles. Ethelred was to recognise his brother as a saint in 1001, in an attempt at posthumous reconciliation, but treacherous nobles used the mythology surrounding the murdered king as partial justification for disloyalty.

During the mid-980s Ethelred assumed responsibility for the governance of England, and married Elgiva, the daughter of a nobleman. Ethelred and Elgiva were destined to become the parents of six sons and five daughters. The sons were named Athelstan, Edmund, Edgar, Edred, Edwy, and Egbert. Three of the daughters were Edith, Elgiva, and Wulfhilda, but the names of the others are no longer known. Ethelred understandably distrusted the nobility, and was unwilling to take advice. This was the source of the name Ethelred "the Unready", a later mistranslation of "Ethelred Unraed", the phrase coined during his reign. The name Ethelred meant "noble counsel", while Unraed meant "no counsel". The nickname referred to the way in which Ethelred frequently took important decisions without consulting the Witan, while also reflecting the fact that the nobility often failed to provide him with support. Ethelred's rule was also undermined by apparent inconsistency, as policy swung between appeasement of enemies and savage repression.

Amidst mistrust and uncertainty, Ethelred battled to defend England, as sporadic Danish attacks during the 980s were followed by regular invasions in the next decade. In both 991 and 994, Ethelred paid the Danish army a large amount of money, known as Danegeld, to leave England. In 1000, during a respite from these invasions, Ethelred led English attacks on Strathclyde and the Isle of Man. The Danes returned in 1001, and left again in the early part of the following year, receiving a third payment of Danegeld.

Elgiva, Ethelred's wife, died at Winchester in February 1002, and he immediately arranged to marry Emma, the sister of Richard II, Duke of Normandy. The marriage took place at Winchester Cathedral on April 5 1002, following which Ethelred and Emma had two sons, Edward – who became King Edward "the Confessor" – and Alfred, as well as a daughter, named Goda. In the course of his two marriages, Ethelred fathered 14 children, with all eight of his sons being named after men among his predecessors as kings of Wessex and England.

In November 1002 Ethelred organised the massacre of many of the Danes living in England, in a failed attempt to end the influence of their fellow settlers. Gunhilda, a sister of Swein "Forkbeard", king of

Denmark since 985, was among those murdered, and the event provoked a further Danish invasion, which took place the following year. The next Danish incursion was launched in 1006, and halted in 1007 by a payment of Danegeld. Each time they received payment. the Danes promised peace, only to carry out another attack, as they sought further plunder.

The *Anglo-Saxon Chronicle* entry for 1009 writes that the Danes "ravaged and burnt, as is their custom, everywhere in Sussex and Hampshire, and also in Berkshire". This was a sustained onslaught, with the Danish army remaining in England until 1012, showing a military superiority that undermined English morale, before leaving in return for a huge payment of Danegeld. In 1013 Swein, supported by his son Cnut, carried out a new invasion, securing control of the Danelaw, followed by the surrender of Winchester and London. At the end of the year the nobility accepted Swein as king of England, while Ethelred fled from London to the Isle of Wight, where he spent Christmas, before taking refuge in Normandy.

Swein died in February 1014, and Ethelred returned, promising the nobility that his rule would be more just. During 1015, Cnut conquered Wessex, while Ethelred's son, Edmund, took control in part of the Danelaw, following a rift with the king. At the start of 1016, Cnut invaded the Danelaw, and Ethelred was reconciled with Edmund, as they planned to defend London together. The strain of events and illness, overwhelmed Ethelred, who died in London on April 23, aged around 47. The *Chronicle* reflected "He ended his days on St George's Day, and he had held the kingdom with great toil and difficulties as long as his life lasted". Ethelred was king for 38 years, apart from an interval of a few weeks, making his reign the longest of any Anglo-Saxon monarch, and he remains one of the few English sovereigns to have both lost and regained the throne.

A meeting of nobles, in London, proclaimed Edmund as king, but the Wessex nobility, assembled at Southampton, recognised Cnut. Edmund's prompt coronation, at the Church of St Paul the Apostle, was the first such event to take place in London. Cnut continued his military campaign, and achieved a significant victory in a battle against Edmund at Ashingdon, in Essex, during October. Edmund and Cnut agreed to partition England, with the former ruling in Wessex, while the latter would control the rest of the country. This awkward arrangement ended with the death of Edmund, on November 30, following which Cnut was accepted as undisputed king of England, despite being a Danish invader, and young man – aged about 21. On January 6 1017, Cnut's position was confirmed, with a coronation at the church where Edmund had received the same recognition.

Cnut swiftly removed potential rivals, arranging the murder, or exile, of several members of the English royal family and nobility. At the same time, he married Emma of Normandy, the widow of Ethelred. Besides the rulers of Denmark and Normandy sharing a common Viking ancestry, Cnut was a first cousin of Emma. Cnut married Emma despite having already contracted an uncanonical marriage to Aelfgifu of Northampton, an English woman who had borne him two sons, Swein and Harold. In 1019, Cnut travelled to Denmark, and established himself as king of that nation, following the death of his brother, Harold IV.

Cnut returned to England during 1020, deciding to rule his newly-founded empire from Winchester, which had been established as the national capital by the Anglo-Saxon monarchs. By making Winchester a focal point, rather than Denmark or the Danelaw, Cnut signalled the continuity of his rule as a king of England, rather than the element of conquest. As part of this process, he worked with Wulfstan, the Archbishop of York, on a comprehensive legal code. This code – the longest issued by any king of England prior to the Norman Conquest – was largely a consolidation of the laws of previous monarchs, particularly Edgar and Ethelred. During the latter part of his reign, Cnut's closest advisor was Godwin, Earl of Wessex, an opportunistic Englishman, who was briefly married to Thyra, a sister of Cnut. After the death of Thyra, Godwin married Gytha, a Danish noblewoman. Another of Cnut's leading English allies was Leofric, Earl of Mercia. Leofric was married to Lady Godiva, the woman subsequently reputed to have ridden naked on a horse through Coventry, in a protest against taxes levied by the government of Harthacnut, a son of Cnut and Emma.

Cnut is often referred to as Canute, the latter being an Anglicised version of his Danish name. The king sat on a beach and attempting, in vain, to halt the incoming tide is one of the most familiar among the many legends that illuminate British history. The continued potency of the image, nearly a thousand years after the event, contrasts with the slender evidence upon which it is based. This charming anecdote is also the reason for which Cnut is most commonly recalled, despite his place among the most significant early kings of England. Our main source is a brief, and enigmatic, description provided by Henry of Huntingdon, in his twelfth century *History of the English*. Henry had access to sources lost to us, including a supposed transcription of Cnut's actual words. Fragments have also been gathered from other accounts.

Adoring courtiers suggested the sea would respond to the king's commands. Cnut had a throne transported to the beach at Bosham, in what is now West Sussex, and sat commanding the waves to halt before him. As the inevitable advance of the tide brought the waves up to his throne, Cnut announced to those who witnessed the event "Let all men know how empty and worthless is the power of kings, for there is none worthy of the name, but He whom heaven, earth, and sea obey by eternal laws". The king had staged the event to prove that he could not halt the waves, rather than as an attempt to emulate impossible claims. Having pronounced upon the authority of God, Cnut rode to Winchester Cathedral, where he placed his gold crown upon a statue of Jesus Christ on the cross. After making this dramatic gesture, Cnut chose never to wear his crown again.

Cnut developed an affection for his new home that was to become greater than the ties to the land of his birth. His residence in this country is recalled in the names of several roads, including Canute Road in Winchester, and Canute Place in Southampton. The latter is linked to a local belief that the supposed attempt to halt the tide was staged at Southampton, rather than Bosham. Southampton makes sense as a location for the event, being the nearest coastal point to Winchester. The combination of decisiveness, justice, loyalty, and piety displayed by Cnut brought him rapid acceptance as their ruler by the English people. He had built upon military victory, and brought domestic peace to England after the ravages of recent wars. In return for this the English were willing to overlook the fact that Cnut was a foreign conqueror. Cnut actually commanded greater loyalty than several of his predecessors as king of England, for they had struggled to unite a country in which the Danelaw challenged central authority.

Cnut travelled southwards through central Europe during the early part of 1027. The journey, which emphasised Christianity rather than Cnut's standing as a warrior, was a pilgrimage to Rome. He attended the coronation of the Holy Roman Emperor, Conrad II, in a ceremony performed by Pope John XIX, on Easter Sunday. Soon after arriving back in England, Cnut departed with an army on an incursion into Scotland, which strengthened his position in the border region. He received the submission of the current Scottish monarch, Malcolm II (reigned 1005-1034), and a man who would become one of his successors, Macbeth (1040-1057). Malcolm II (a son of Kenneth II) was the last king descended in the male line from Kenneth MacAlpin, who had effectively established the unified Scottish monarchy. Macbeth and his wife, Gruoch, later became the central characters in William Shakespeare's "Scottish Play".

Cnut attempted to guard England against attack from the south, by maintaining the alliance with the Normans, through the marriage of Estrith, his sister, to Robert, Duke of Normandy – son of the recently-deceased Richard II. This plan faltered as Robert repudiated Estrith, preferring the charms of Herleva, his mistress. Norman legend recalls that Robert first saw Herleva (the daughter of a tanner) when she washed her clothes in a stream that flowed past Falaise Castle. Robert and Herleva had an illegitimate son, destined to become William the Conqueror, the first Norman king of England.

In 1028, Cnut led a joint English and Danish conquest of Norway. He had become king of three different lands, and the symbolic – although not literal – master of the northern seas of Europe. Cnut returned to England in 1029, whereupon Hakon, a Norwegian earl and nephew of Cnut, became regent of his newly-conquered homeland. Hakon died the following year, at which point Cnut appointed Aelfgifu, his former English concubine, and their son Swein, as regents in Norway.

Cnut spent the final years of his life quietly in England. Religious contemplation, and bestowal of gifts to the church, became increasingly important to Cnut. He did not seek to intervene as Aelfgifu and Swein were confronted with a growing rebellion in Norway, which led to that country restoring its independence shortly before Cnut died. In 1033, Robert, Duke of Normandy, seriously considered an invasion of England, aimed at making Edward, the son of Ethelred and Emma, the monarch. Robert did not, however, proceed with this paradoxical anticipation of the eventual Norman Conquest. The *Anglo-Saxon Chronicle* entry for 1035 records that "In this year king Cnut died on 12 November at Shaftesbury, and he was brought from there to Winchester, and buried there". Cnut enjoyed a remarkable odyssey, but died aged only about 40.

The theatrics of Cnut's failure to halt the waves on Bosham beach was less important than another role he played, as a central figure in the steadily advancing tide of Danish and Norman invasion. Swein had been the first foreigner to breach the defences of the Anglo-Saxon monarchy, albeit briefly. After Ethelred's restoration, and the short reign of Edmund, the next wave brought a decisive breakthrough, with Cnut as the king. The Danish hold on England continued during the rule of his sons, Harold Harefoot and Harthacnut. A disputed succession, in 1035, led to Harold becoming effective king until his death in 1040, at which point Harthacnut took the throne. Harthacnut was childless, and designated his half-brother Edward as heir. When Harthacnut died in 1042, the accession of Edward returned the House of Wessex to the throne, but the new king had been brought up in Normandy, the home of his mother, Emma, and Normans were to have a major influence at his court. Edward "the Confessor", as he came to be known, followed a strict interpretation of Christianity, and did not indulge in the consummation of his marriage to Edith, a daughter of Godwin. In the absence of any offspring, Edward declared William, the son of his cousin Robert, as heir to the throne. William had succeeded Robert as Duke of Normandy in 1035, despite being only a child, and illegitimate.

To the west, Gruffydd ap Llywelyn was in the process of establishing himself as king of all Cymru / Wales. Gruffydd was the son of Llywelyn ap Seissyll, who had ruled Deheubarth, Gwynedd, and Powys. Gruffydd began his rise by conquering Powys, in 1027. Gwynedd was gained in 1039, a year in which Gruffydd won a battle at Rhyd y Groes, killing Edwin, the brother of Leofric, Earl of Mercia. Gruffydd took control of Deheubarth and Morgannwg in 1055, and was to retain power across Wales until his death. Gruffydd was also involved in struggles across the border in England, forming an alliance with Elfgar of Mercia, a son of Leofric. Gruffydd married Ealdgyth, a daughter of Elfgar. The power of Gruffydd prompted Edward to authorise an attack upon the former's territory. This was headed by Harold Godwinson and Tostig – brothers of Edward's wife, Edith – and led to the death in 1063 of Gruffydd, who was killed by Welsh rebels. Bleddyn ap Cynfyn, a half-brother of Gruffydd, was installed as king of Gwynedd, and ruled until his death in 1073.

William of Normandy envisaged ruling England, but when Edward died, in January 1066, the English chose Harold Godwinson as his successor. Harold had become Earl of Wessex on the death of Godwin in 1053, and claimed to be part of English royalty, as a brother-in-law of the late king. Around the time that he became a monarch, Harold married Ealdgyth, the widow of Gruffydd, the late Welsh king. Harold's brief reign ended with his death at the Battle of Hastings, on October 14 1066, as William and his army – which had sailed across the English Channel in more than 700 ships – began the Norman Conquest. Fifty years after Cnut became king, William the Conqueror brought the final destruction of the Anglo-Saxon monarchy.

Emma of Normandy, a great aunt of William, had taken the unusual step, for a woman in the eleventh century, of commissioning a biography of herself. The *Encomium Emmae Reginae*, written around 1041, exalted Cnut and Emma, with the author – an anonymous monk from Flanders – refusing to allow the facts to get in the way of a good story, and omitting to mention Emma's marriage to Ethelred. Emma was a brave and resourceful woman, who exerted intermittent influence on English politics over several decades, while coping with spells of exile or ostracism. Genealogical symmetry made Emma the wife of two kings (Ethelred and Cnut), the mother of two kings (Harthacnut and Edward), and the stepmother of two kings (Edmund and Harold Harefoot). Emma died at Winchester in 1052, half a century after she married Ethelred in that city, and was buried there alongside Cnut. The bones of the Danish king, and Norman queen, were subsequently interred in a group of mortuary chests at Winchester Cathedral, as were the remains of several Anglo-Saxon monarchs, including Egbert, and bishops. In 1642 the mortuary chests were ransacked by Puritans, during the Civil War, and the bones became mixed up. During 2014, the cathedral announced work was underway on attempted DNA identification. Pending developments, the bones of Cnut remain combined with those of a number of native English kings. This rather gruesome arrangement is strangely symbolic, as Cnut interrupted the established order in Anglo-Saxon England, and secured an ironic position in our national tradition.

5 Domesday Book and Magna Carta

We have reached 1066, a point midway through the recorded history of England and Britain. After the Normans won the Battle of Hastings, William the Conqueror – a nickname apparently developed a few decades after his death – marched to London, and was crowned king at Westminster Abbey, on Christmas Day. The territory of England had been conquered for the fourth time in less than a thousand years, with the Romans, Anglo-Saxons, and Vikings now being followed by the Normans. In the immediate aftermath of the death of Harold, Edgar the Atheling, a grandson of King Edmund, attempted to challenge William for the throne. During 1068, Bleddyn ap Cynfyn, ruler of Gwynedd, and his brother, Rhiwallon, joined an unsuccessful English and Welsh resistance to William the Conqueror, which was led by Edwin, Earl of Mercia, and Morcar, Earl of Northumbria. Eight centuries later, Edwin and Morcar, who were sons of Elfgar of Mercia, would be mentioned in *Alice's Adventures in Wonderland* (1865) by Lewis Carroll – as material from a history book is recited.

The lack of native success in countering the Norman Conquest led to the English seeking assistance from Swein Estrithson, king of Denmark, who was a nephew of Cnut. With hopes for a revival of the Anglo-Danish empire, Swein Estrithson invaded England in 1069, in an attempt to depose William, but agreed a peace the following year. Edgar the Atheling was reconciled with William shortly afterwards. William's Norman supporters were rewarded with ownership of nearly all the land in England, in return for formal allegiance to the king, in what became known as the Feudal System. William commissioned a massive survey of land, resources, and value, carried out during 1086. The planning for this Domesday Book is recorded in the *Anglo-Saxon Chronicle* entry for the preceding year – linking two contrasting records of England.

The king had a large meeting, and very deep consultation with his council, about this land, how it was occupied, and by what sort of men. Then sent he his men over all England into each shire, commissioning them to find out "How many hundreds of hides were in the shire, what land the king himself had, and what stock upon the land, or, what dues he ought to have by the year from the shire". Also he commissioned them to record in writing "How much land his archbishops had, and his diocesan bishops, and his abbots, and his earls", and though I may be prolix and tedious, "What, or how much, each man had, who was an occupier of land in England, either in land or in stock, and how much money it was worth".

The report did not actually have a title, but was known in the twelfth century as the Book of Winchester, as it was usually deposited in the relevant city. It subsequently became Domesday Book – an allusion to both the English word "doom", meaning a law or judgement, and the Biblical Last Judgement. The name Domesday Book was first used in an official document in 1221, at which time its importance was being matched by Magna Carta, a legal agreement signed as recently as 1215. As for the *Anglo-Saxon Chronicle*, work continued through the Norman period, with the final entry, written by a monk at Peterborough Abbey, covering the events of 1154. The 1086 inquiry did not attempt to quantify the actual population of England, but modern research suggests that around two million people lived in the country at that point – similar to the total for all of Britain when the Romans arrived, a thousand years earlier. The vast majority of these people continued to speak English during the Norman period. The next few centuries saw an increasing assimilation of French words into the English language.

When William died in 1087, his eldest son, Robert, became Duke of Normandy. The English crown passed to the Conqueror's second surviving son, William II, nicknamed Rufus, the Latin word for red, due to his having hair of that colour as a child. During 1088, a rebellion by Norman nobles within England attempted to depose William, and install Robert as king, but the latter man did not join the insurrection, and it failed. William in turn invaded Normandy in 1091, seizing some land from Robert.

William Rufus organised the building of Westminster Hall, in 1097, as part of the Palace of Westminster. The palace and Westminster Abbey were built in the middle of the century, by Edward the Confessor. Nowadays Westminster Hall is the oldest surviving part of the Palace of Westminster, home of the Houses of Parliament. Most of the palace was destroyed by a fire, in 1834, following which the majority of the current Parliament building was slowly constructed, between 1840 and 1870. Strengthening control in England, the Normans built a series of impressive castles, including the Tower of London – on the north bank of the Thames, in the east of the city of London. The Tower of London served as one of the principal royal residences for several centuries, before becoming a notorious Tudor prison. In the present day, the Tower officially remains a royal palace, which is open as a tourist attraction.

William II was killed, during 1100, in an apparent hunting accident in the New Forest – there has been speculation it may have been murder. The supposed spot of the king's death is now marked by a monument, Rufus Stone. William II was succeeded as king of England by his younger brother, Henry I, who soon married Matilda, a daughter of Malcolm III, king of Scotland. Matilda carried the blood of the Anglo-

Saxon monarchy, and this strengthened Henry's position as ruler of England. He went on to capture Normandy, in 1106, deposing Robert. Henry continued a policy of both preceding Norman kings, with military intervention in Scotland and Wales, aiming to assert England as the dominant state in Britain.

Henry I fathered more than twenty children, with a series of mistresses, but died in 1135 without a legitimate male heir. Henry and Matilda's son, William, had drowned in 1120, being one of about 250 people killed when the White Ship sank off the coast of Normandy. Henry subsequently designated his legitimate daughter, also named Matilda, as heiress. Matilda was married to Henry V, Holy Roman Emperor, but he died in 1125. When Henry I died, Matilda lacked support at the English court, and Stephen of Blois, a son of the Conqueror's daughter, Adela, seized control of both England and Normandy. Matilda invaded England in 1139, starting a civil war with Stephen, which was to continue for most of his reign. In the late nineteenth century, historians coined the phrase "the Anarchy" to describe this era.

Matilda initially achieved military success, and had herself declared queen in 1141, but was unable to confirm this with a coronation, as Stephen regained the initiative. The conflict stretched to Normandy, and Geoffrey, Count of Anjou, the second husband of Matilda, became Duke of Normandy, by conquest, in 1144. Peace was eventually reached in England in 1153, when the Treaty of Winchester confirmed Stephen as king for the remainder of his lifetime, in return for his being succeeded by Henry, the son of Matilda – rather than Stephen's son William. Stephen died in 1154, and Matilda's son duly became King Henry II. Matilda spent the latter years of her eventful life in Normandy, where she helped Henry to govern, and died at Rouen in 1167.

The reign of Henry II (1154-1189) ushered in a new era, with the House of Plantagenet destined to rule for over three hundred years. This remains the longest tenure for any of the sub-families within the history of the English monarchy. Plantagenet originated as a nickname for Geoffrey V, Count of Anjou, the father of Henry II. The adoption of Plantagenet as a surname for the English royal family did not, however, occur until the fifteenth century, when it was taken by Richard, Third Duke of York, the father of both Edward IV and Richard III. Historians have retrospectively applied the name Plantagenet to all English kings from 1154 to 1485.

Initially the rule of the Plantagenets continued the Norman and French influence but, with the passage of time, the family became more English. Nevertheless the Plantagenets sought to retain, and expand, their power within France. Henry II built up a mass of territory, either side of the

English Channel, subsequently known as the Angevin Empire. Besides the inheritance of England, via his mother, Matilda, Henry succeeded to the territories of Geoffrey, Count of Anjou. Henry's marriage to Eleanor of Aquitaine, which took place in 1152, led to his acquisition of Aquitaine. Henry had direct control of more land in France than the reigning French monarch, Louis VII (1137-1180) – who had previously married, and divorced, Eleanor. As well as being a powerful monarch, Henry II was a prolific sire. Besides eight legitimate children, borne by Eleanor, Henry had several mistresses, and at least a dozen illegitimate children. Henry's first legitimate son, William, Count of Poitiers, died as an infant in 1156, the year after the birth of the second son, Henry. Richard, the third legitimate son, born in 1157, was followed in 1158 by Geoffrey, Duke of Brittany. The youngest of Henry II's legitimate children was John, born in 1167, destined to become king of England. In 1170 Henry II had his son Henry crowned in England, in expectation of the latter eventually succeeding to the kingdom. Thereafter the son was known as "the Young King".

Richard I is one of the most famous of English monarchs, and commonly referred to as "the Lionheart", but the reputation is at odds with his record as a king. He was born in 1157, at Oxford, but from 1165 onwards much of his childhood was spent in France. Richard lived with his mother, Eleanor, who was now effectively separated from Henry II. During 1172 Richard was proclaimed Duke of Aquitaine, in a ceremony at Poitiers. The influence of Eleanor (a cultured woman who did much to popularise Arthurian legend) imbued Richard with a love of learning, and he showed interest in both music and poetry. French was Richard's main language, and he never learnt English.

Plantagenet family fable held that an early count of Anjou married a beautiful and mysterious woman, whom he brought home from travels in a far away land. The woman always left mass early, until one day the count, suspicious of this behaviour, arranged for knights to bar his wife's exit. When the countess beheld Holy Communion for the first time, she supposedly screamed, and found the strength to literally fly away from church, never to be seen again. The people of Anjou concluded that the woman was the embodiment of Melusine, the daughter of Satan. The Plantagenets had a fiery temper, and tendency towards conflict among themselves, attributed to the influence of infernal ancestry, becoming known as "the Devil's brood".

In 1173 Henry "the Young King", Richard, and Geoffrey launched a rebellion against their father. After sporadic fighting in both England and France, Henry II survived the onslaught, and agreed a peace with his sons in 1174. Eleanor of Aquitaine was now taken to England by Henry II, and held as a prisoner, until her release upon the death of the king.

Eleanor's was detained at a series of locations, including Old Sarum, a settlement in Wiltshire, which was moved two miles south to form Salisbury during the next century. The death, in 1183, of Henry "the Young King" left Richard as heir to the Angevin Empire. Richard, being impatient to gain power, worked with Philippe II of France (1180-1223) against Henry II in 1187. John subsequently joined this alliance, breaking the spirit of Henry II, who died on July 6 1189.

Richard rapidly visited both Normandy, where he was accepted as duke, and England, establishing himself as king, with a coronation at Westminster Abbey on September 3. Richard was gripped by the idea of joining a planned Christian crusade, aimed at regaining control of Jerusalem, which had been captured by Muslims, led by Saladin, the Sultan of Egypt and Syria, in 1187. Richard's main preoccupation while in England was the raising of funds for the crusade – he said "I would sell London, if I could find anybody rich enough to buy it". In December 1189, Richard returned to France.

Richard prepared his role in what became the Third Crusade with Philippe, and the two men departed France together, in July 1190. Reaching Sicily a few weeks later, they became involved in a domestic power struggle, which lasted several months. The peace agreement, in March 1191, between Richard, Philippe, and Tancred, king of Sicily, included an exchange of gifts. Richard gave Tancred a sword, proclaimed to be King Arthur's Excalibur, swapping a supposedly precious piece of England's heritage for a fleet of Sicilian ships, to move men and supplies for the crusade.

Eleanor, who wished to gain Navarre as an ally for Aquitaine, suggested that Richard marry Berengaria of Navarre, and he agreed. After a stop at Rhodes, Richard arrived in Cyprus, and married Berengaria at St George's Chapel in Limassol, on May 12 1191. Richard reached the Holy Land in June, finding this a mystical place, and apparently witnessed a vision of Saint George. Acre was captured from Muslim control in July 1191, with Richard taking part in the battle despite being laid low by scurvy – it was said that he used his crossbow while being carried on a stretcher. The crusaders took 2,700 Muslim prisoners at Acre, and these were brutally murdered on the orders of Richard. The crusaders were soon divided by disputes between the English, French, and Germans. Philippe returned to France, and Saladin successfully defended Jerusalem. On September 2 1192, Richard concluded a peace with Saladin.

During the journey home bad weather in the Mediterranean caused Richard to be shipwrecked, forcing him to travel overland through hostile territory. Richard was captured, near Vienna, by Leopold V of Austria, with whom he had clashed during the crusade. Leopold handed his prisoner over to Henry VI, the Holy Roman Emperor, who held Richard in Germany, and demanded a ransom of 150,000 marks – equivalent to five times the annual income of the English crown. The ransom was raised within England, largely due to the efforts of Eleanor of Aquitaine, and Richard was released on February 4 1194. The imprisonment of Richard gave rise to a famous legend, which begins with Richard and Margery, a daughter of Henry VI, falling in love. Henry decided to kill Richard by sending a hungry lion into the latter's cell. Margery told Richard of the plan, and he asked her to provide forty silk handkerchiefs, which were then bound around his right arm. Magically empowered by Margery's silk, Richard put a hand into the lion's mouth, and down into its body, killing it by tearing out the animal's heart. Richard displayed the heart to Henry, before eating it. This supposed incident, rather than his general courage in battle, earned Richard the nickname "Lionheart" – which originated as the French phrase "Coeur de Lion".

Richard returned to England following his release, landing at Sandwich on March 13 1194. With John having sought to seize control during Richard's absence, the king re-asserted his authority, being crowned for a second time. Whereas Richard's first coronation had taken place at Westminster, the repeat event was staged at Winchester Cathedral, on April 17. A few days later, the king travelled to Portsmouth, where he prepared to depart for France. During his short stay, Richard initiated construction that began the process whereby Portsmouth became one of the nation's leading naval bases. Richard sailed on May 12, and was destined never to return to England.

In France, Richard had the better of extensive fighting against Philippe, regaining territory that had been seized during the captivity. During 1197 and 1198, Richard oversaw the building of the imposing castle of Chateau-Gaillard, towering high above the River Seine at Les Andelys, as a defence for Normandy. Chateau-Gaillard was French for Saucy Castle, with the literal meaning of saucy being impudent behaviour. Richard's fortification of Les Andelys defied a provision of a peace treaty agreed with Philippe, at Louviers, in 1196. Richard made the castle his main home from the time of its erection, as he fell in love with the place, also referring to it as the "fair castle of the rock".

Ahead of his victory over Philippe at the Battle of Gisors, fought on September 27 1198, Richard coined the motto "Dieu et Mon Droit", which meant "God and My Right". Richard was asserting that he held his titles by the divine right of kings, as opposed to temporal arrangements, by which his control of land within France was subject to the overlordship of the king of France. The phrase "Dieu et Mon Droit" has continued to be used as a motto by English and British monarchs ever since then. A few months earlier, in May 1198, Richard launched a new seal for the English crown, as a financial expedient amidst mounting debts caused by his wars – the monarch simply repudiating obligations made under his previous seal. The 1198 seal included the three lions, a motif that has become a permanent fixture in English history. The three lions have provided the badge on the shirt of the England football team, since the first ever international match, a 0-0 draw with Scotland, at Glasgow, on Saint Andrew's Day 1872.

At the start of 1199, Richard became involved in a dispute over a hoard of gold, apparently left by the Romans, found at Chalus, in Aquitaine. Richard besieged the castle of Chalus-Chabrol, and was wounded by an arrow fired from the castle. Gangrene set into the wound, and Richard died on April 6, aged 41, with his mother in attendance. A few days before he died, Richard named John his successor as king of England, despite the latter having regularly rebelled. Richard had called Eleanor to his death bed, but not his wife. Berengaria had not spent any time in England during her eight years as queen consort, but made a few visits after his death, became a nun, settled in France, and lived for more than thirty years after the death of Richard. His body was buried at Fontevraud Abbey, in Anjou, alongside that of Henry II – Eleanor would later be buried there. Richard directed that his heart be interred at Roeun in Normandy, while his bowels were buried at Charroux in Aquitaine, in response to Richard's perception that Aquitaine had been disloyal to him. In this division of his remains, Richard excluded England.

Richard exerted an international influence that stretched much further, in geographical terms, than any of his predecessors among England's monarchs. Much romanticism surrounding Richard stems from misplaced stories of Robin Hood, set in the reigns of Richard and John. Historical research has demonstrated that the real-life Robin Hood lived in the thirteenth century, while Richard spent very little time, during the twelfth century, in England, but fiction often juxtaposes the two men.

The barbarity of the crusade has often been overlooked in this country. In the Middle East, however, Richard's role has often been recalled with more accuracy. During the thirteenth century, Arab mothers would attempt to quell unruly children with the suggestion that "King Richard will get you". Richard is still cast as a demon in anti-Western propaganda. In 1991, exactly 800 years after Richard fought in the Third Crusade, the first Gulf War saw an international coalition, led by the USA and Britain, end the Iraqi occupation of Kuwait, which had been invaded the previous year. The invasion was ordered by Saddam Hussein, who had been born in Tikrit, a town in Iraq which had also been the birthplace of Saladin. A few days after Al-Qaeda attacked the USA, on September 11 2001, President George W Bush called his war against terrorism "a crusade". Bush was widely criticised for this unfortunate comparison, especially as he was seeking support within the Middle East against Al-Qaeda and Osama Bin Laden.

The second Gulf War, in 2003, resulted in the downfall of Saddam Hussein's regime in Iraq. The occupying military force from the USA captured Saddam Hussein, at the end of that year. It was, however, the state of Iraq which tried and executed Saddam, in 2006, for murders committed by his regime. Long before the principle was established that a tyrannical head of state, such as Saddam Hussein, could be held responsible for his crimes by international opinion, Richard instigated the massacre at Acre, during the Third Crusade. For several years, Britain's role in the second Gulf War, and the ongoing military presence in Iraq, remained controversial, with public debate bitterly contested. There is a statue of Richard outside the Houses of Parliament, sat on horseback, and riding into battle. The statue, which has stood since 1860 as an embodiment of British history, is a replica of a piece made for the Great Exhibition of 1851. The statue was crafted by Carlo Marochetti, a sculptor born in Italy, raised as a Frenchman, and exiled in England after the revolution that forced the abdication of King Louis-Philippe of France in 1848. The placement of this statue of Richard was paradoxical, given his minor role within England, during a lifetime that preceded the establishment of Parliament. The choice of Marochetti as sculptor was strangely appropriate, for Richard was essentially a Frenchman born outside of France.

Much of the Angevin territory, which King Richard held in France, was lost by John (1199-1216). John's incompetent rule within England led to a rebellion by the barons, who took control of London in 1215. On June 15, at Runnymede in Surrey, John signed an agreement with the barons, named Magna Carta – this was Latin for "Great Paper". Runnymede had previously been the location for meetings of the Witan, called by King Alfred, in the late ninth century. Multiple copies of Magna Carta were written, and distributed to government officials around the country. Four copies from 1215 have survived to the present day – two being held at the British Library, while the others are at Lincoln Castle, and Salisbury Cathedral respectively. Only one copy, at the British Library, has an original seal, but both the seal and the paper were damaged by a fire in 1731, leaving the document virtually illegible.

The document set out limitations to royal power, and codified the rights of the nobility. There were also supposed rights for ordinary people, but centuries were to pass before they succeeded in asserting these, through radical political pressure. Large parts of Magna Carta were copied, with little change, from a Charter of Liberties, issued by Henry I in 1100. The main new provision was clause 61, the "security clause", which provided for the establishment of a council of 25 barons, with the right to over-rule the monarch. John soon attempted to revoke the charter, saying he had agreed it under duress. John was supported by Pope Innocent III, with the later realising that baronial rights that would reduce influence of the Catholic Church over the monarchy.

John's decision to renege on his agreement provoked a conflict, known as the First Barons' War. The barons invited Louis, son of Philippe II of France, to invade England, to protect their liberties from John. Louis arrived in May 1216, and within a few weeks had captured both London and Winchester, before conquering a large part of England, and being proclaimed king by the barons. John died on October 18 1216. being succeeded by his son, Henry III, aged nine. The following month, the royal government, set up as regents for Henry, confirmed Magna Carta, in his name, but with some clauses omitted. War continued after the death of John. Louis abandoned his attempt to be king of England – he was subsequently Louis VIII of France. After peace was agreed, the government repeated the reissue of Magna Carta, in late 1217. Henry III issued a shortened version of the agreement in 1225, on becoming an adult. Henry later concluded the Treaty of Paris, with Louis IX of France, in 1259, accepting the loss of the Angevin Empire, with the exception of Aquitaine.

Rebellion against the monarchy continued, and the Second Barons' War was fought between 1264 and 1267. This led to the calling of England's first elected Parliament, held from January to March 1265, on the initiative of Simon de Montfort, Sixth Earl of Leicester. De Montfort had been born in France, a great grandson of Alice Fitzroy, an illegitimate daughter of Henry I. De Montfort had previously been an ally of Henry III, and married the king's sister, Eleanor, in 1238. De Montfort was killed in August 1265, at the Battle of Evesham. The first electorate was restricted to men, who either owned land in a county area, or had influence in one of a limited number of boroughs, while women were excluded. This qualification for the franchise, falling far short of democracy, remained largely unchanged from 1265 until 1832 – the first 567 years of the English / British Parliament. The name Parliament developed from the French "parlement", meaning a talking place. The Parliament of Scotland was also founded during the thirteenth century, with the modern archive for the institution tracing the event to 1235. In that year, a meeting of a group similar to the council which advised the monarch was described as a "Colloquium", a word equivalent to Parliament. The name Parliament began to be used for the Scottish body during 1293.

Henry III remained king of England for 56 years, dying in 1272, and being succeeded by a son, Edward I, who was to reissue the 1225 version of Magna Carta, in 1297. During the fourteenth and fifteenth centuries, the document was regularly reconfirmed, by monarchs and Parliament. Three clauses, from the 1297 version, remain part of current British law:

1 We have granted to God, and by this our present Charter have confirmed, for Us and our Heirs for ever, that the Church of England shall be free, and shall have all her whole Rights and Liberties inviolable. We have granted also, and given to all the Freemen of our Realm, for Us and our Heirs for ever, these Liberties under-written, to have and to hold to them and their Heirs, of Us and our Heirs for ever.

9 The City of London shall have all the old Liberties and Customs which it hath been used to have. Moreover We will and grant, that all other Cities, Boroughs, Towns, and the Barons of the Five Ports, as with all other Ports, shall have all their Liberties and free Customs.

29 No Freeman shall be taken or imprisoned, or be disseised of his Freehold, or Liberties, or free Customs, or be outlawed, or exiled, or any other wise destroyed; nor will We not pass upon him, nor condemn him, but by lawful judgment of his Peers, or by the Law of the land. We will sell to no man, we will not deny or defer to any man either Justice or Right.

During 2015, events were held to mark the eight hundredth anniversary of the original document, led by the Magna Carta Trust. The organisation had been set up in October 1956, receiving a letter of support from Anthony Eden, the Prime Minister, who wrote:

The granting of Magna Carta marked the road to individual freedom, to Parliamentary democracy and to the supremacy of the law. The principles of Magna Carta, developed over the centuries by the Common Law, are the heritage now, not only of those who live in these Islands, but in countless millions of all races and creeds throughout the world. It is most fitting that a Trust should be formed to commemorate so great a moment in history, and I send my best wishes for your success.

At the time, Eden was planning a "moment in history", which led to his notorious reputation. This was military action against Egypt, attempting to end the Suez crisis. Eden pursued this in defiance of a declaration from the United Nations, a body trying to uphold an international "supremacy of the law". Eden soon had to accept a humiliating failure to defeat Egypt, amidst the decline of the British Empire.

6 The Late Middle Ages

Events in England were increasingly intertwined with those in Scotland, and Wales, during the period we know as the Late Middle Ages. Edward I (1272-1307) was the first English king with that name to rule after the Norman Conquest. The three Edwards who were monarchs in the Anglo-Saxon era – recalled as "the Elder", "the Martyr", and "the Confessor" respectively – have not been given regnal numbers. Edward I was the first English monarch to display the flag of Saint George, with the red cross on a white background symbolising blood spilt in the crucifixion of Jesus Christ. Edward wished to expand his power across Britain, and led an English conquest of Wales, between 1277 and 1283. Llywelyn ap Gruffudd, a member of the royal family of Gwynedd, recognised from 1258 as Prince of Wales – the foremost leader in the territory – was killed in battle in 1282. Edward I had his son, the future Edward II, declared Prince of Wales in 1301. This began the continuing tradition of the heir to the English, and now British, crown being known as the Prince of Wales.

Edward I intervened in Scotland, taking advantage of his role as mediator in a disputed succession to the throne, following the death of Margaret "Maid of Norway", a child who was nominal queen of Scotland from 1286 until 1290. The Scottish crown was awarded to John Balliol in 1292, but he was deposed in 1296, following an English invasion. Edward I quickly subjugated Scotland but, during the reign of Edward II (1307-1327), the Scots fought back, led by Robert Bruce (1306-1329). According to legend, following defeat in a battle, Robert Bruce hid in a cave, and considered fleeing from Scotland. Seeing a spider persist in efforts to build a web, and finally succeed, Bruce resolved to continue the military effort. A subsequent victory at the Battle of Bannockburn, in 1314, enabled Scotland to regain its independence.

Dissatisfaction among the English nobility with Edward II led to his being deposed by Parliament, and replaced by his son, Edward III (1327-1377), who launched a war, seeking to claim the French crown. The requirement for taxation, to finance the conflict, enabled Parliament to increase its influence. From 1341, it sat in two separate rooms, with the elected element being the House of Commons. The unelected house featured the nobility, and senior members of the clergy – becoming known as the House of Lords in 1544. The Hundred Years War, fought at intervals between 1337 and 1453, strengthened the English cult of Saint George. Courageous defeat of an imaginary dragon made George an ideal figurehead, with the nation locked in protracted war against France. Edward III owned a relic of George's blood, and oversaw effective recognition of him as England's patron saint. The previous joint holders of that honour lacked military prowess. Edmund, king of East Anglia (854-869) was tortured, and killed, by Danes who conquered his territory, while Edward "the Confessor" was an exceptionally pious man.

In 1348 Edward III founded the Order of the Garter, which brought together English knights in an attempt to recreate Arthurian romance. The order owed much to the inspiration of Saint George, and Edward created Saint George's Chapel, at Windsor Castle, as a meeting place for its members. The first formal meeting took place on Saint George's Day in 1349. The naming of the order stemmed from a ball held by the English court in France in 1347, during a lengthy siege of Calais, which followed Edward leading his army to victory in the Battle of Crecy, during the previous year. Although Edward III was married to Philippa of Hainault – in the Holy Roman Empire – he apparently had what would now be called a crush on his cousin, Joan, who was nicknamed the "Fair Maid of Kent", due to the combination of her being the daughter of Edmund, Earl of Kent (a son of Edward I) and her beauty. Joan was also married, in fact she had wedded two men in quick succession, Thomas Holland and William Montague, the latter being both Earl of Salisbury and king of the Isle of Man. The bigamous nature of Joan's second marriage led to it being annulled. Following the death of Thomas Holland, Joan would marry Edward "the Black Prince", a son of Edward III, given the nickname as he carried a black shield in battles. During a dance at the Calais ball, one of the blue silk garters that Joan was wearing to keep her stockings in place fell to the floor, and was immediately retrieved by Edward III, who in turn tied the garter around one of his legs. Amidst suggestive comment from onlookers about his action, Edward declared "Honi soit qui mal y pense", a French phrase meaning "Shame on him who thinks shameful thoughts". The French wording features on the Lion and the Unicorn emblem of the United Kingdom, along with the "Dieu et Mon Droit" motto. This emblem originated with the union of the monarchies of England and Scotland, in 1603. The lion reflects the three lions of England, while the unicorn was a traditional symbol of Scotland, included in the royal coat of arms by King William I (1165-1214). A Unicorn design also featured on Scottish coins during the reigns of James III, James IV, and James V, in the fifteenth and sixteenth centuries.

Saint George's Chapel is an enduring legacy of George's elevation to be England's patron saint. The chapel created by Edward III was rebuilt by his great great grandson Edward IV, with work commencing in 1475. Edward IV was the first king to be buried in the chapel, followed by Henry VIII, Charles I, George III, George IV, William IV, Edward VII, George V, and George VI. Four of the six kings named George have been entombed in the chapel. George I died during a visit to Germany, and his burial took place in Hanover, making him the first English monarch to be buried abroad since Richard I. George II was laid to rest in Westminster Abbey. Royal consorts buried in the chapel include Edward IV's widow, Elizabeth Woodville, and Jane Seymour, the third wife of Henry VIII. In 2002, the body of Queen Elizabeth, the Queen Mother, was buried alongside that of her husband George VI, fifty years after his death. The ashes of Princess Margaret, a daughter of George and Elizabeth, who died a few weeks before the Queen Mother, were also interred in Saint George's Chapel. More recently, Prince Philip, Duke of Edinburgh, and Elizabeth II were buried in the chapel, during 2021 and 2022 respectively.

The Peasants' Revolt stands in British history as the first challenge to the established order by an organised popular movement. The immediate cause of the revolt was the collection, during 1381, of a Poll Tax, levied by the English Parliament the previous year. This followed earlier Poll Taxes, charged in 1377 and 1379, to finance the Hundred Years War. Edward III died in 1377, the year after his eldest son, Edward "the Black Prince", and the throne passed to Richard II, a 10 year old son of the latter. The 1380 tax was particularly iniquitous, as it was three times as heavy as that of 1377, and charged at a flat rate of one shilling per adult, whereas its predecessor had taken some account of people's ability to pay. The underlying grievance of the peasants was villeinage, the manner in which they were controlled by the English feudal system. The Black Death, a plague which is estimated to have killed half of the population of Europe, decimated England during 1348 and 1349. Amidst the resulting scarcity of labour, peasants started to command higher pay until Parliament, under the control of landowners, passed legislation that restricted wages. These same landowners used their position as lords of the manor to compel peasants to perform forced labour. There was also a strong religious element in the revolt, inspired by the ideas of John Wycliffe, who had criticised the abuses of the established church.

    The rebellion started in Essex, during May 1381, as the people of three villages – Fobbing, Corringham, and Stanford-le-Hope – openly defied a government official, appointed to oversee the collection of the Poll Tax. The Essex peasantry attacked manor houses, including Cressing Temple, which belonged to Sir Robert Hales, the Lord Treasurer in the government. A similar uprising arose among the Kent peasantry, led by Wat Tyler, and they marched to London, aiming to put their demands before Richard II. The peasants paraded the flag of Saint George, asserting that the patron saint belonged to the English people as a whole, and not just the monarchy. An estimated 100,000 protestors converged on London, with the Essex men assembling at Mile End, just east of the city, on June 12, and the Kent contingent camping at Blackheath, to the south of the Thames, on the following day. The growing rebellion led to Richard II, now aged 14, being moved from Windsor to the apparent safety of the Tower of London, where he was accompanied by members of the government, and royal household.

The Kent and Essex rebels, joined by London labourers, went on the rampage, attacking various buildings that represented authority, including Lambeth Palace (residence of the Archbishop of Canterbury). They also plundered homes of the wealthy and powerful. One of the houses destroyed was Savoy Palace, residence of John of Gaunt, First Duke of Lancaster, an uncle of Richard II. The insurgents advanced to the Tower of London, shouting their demands to the king, who promised that he would meet with them. At Mile End, on June 14, the peasants, led by Tyler, greeted Richard with pledges of loyalty, and presented him with a petition, seeking the abolition of villeinage, and the right to rent land at four pennies an acre. Richard announced that he would meet these demands. Most of the Essex peasants returned home immediately after the meeting, believing their cause was won.

Thousands of peasants remained outside the Tower, during Richard's encounter with their comrades. They spotted Simon of Sudbury (who combined the role of Archbishop of Canterbury with being Chancellor in the king's government) attempting to escape. As Simon of Sudbury retreated into the Tower, peasants invaded, ransacking the kitchens, bedchambers, and armoury. They forced their way into the apartment of the king's mother, smashed furniture and decorations, and cut up the bedclothes. The king's mother, Joan, the "Fair Maid of Kent", was able to escape the Tower, with the assistance of her attendants, but the rebels captured several men, including Simon of Sudbury, Sir Robert Hales, and John Legge, the latter of whom had been the architect of the Poll Tax. In a brutal parody of the monarchy's execution of traitors at Tower Hill, the peasants took the captured men to that spot, and beheaded them. Rioting continued, including the burning of Highbury Manor, a residence of Hales, organised by Jack Straw, who emerged as one of the leading rebels.

The progress being made by the peasants from Kent and Essex was rapidly communicated throughout England, and prompted a series of allied rebellions. At St Albans, in Hertfordshire, peasants demanded reduction of the manorial rights of Thomas de la Mare, the local abbot. The St Albans rebels, led by William Grindcob, went to London, and put their case to both Richard II, probably at the Mile End meeting, and Tyler. The king granted the requested charter, while Tyler offered to send 20,000 Kentishmen to St Albans if the peasants' demands were not immediately met. Buoyed up by this double endorsement, the St Albans peasants immediately returned home, and attacked the Abbey on June 15. The rebels broke through the gates to the abbot's land, drained the fishpond, and killed the game animals. The peasants then burnt the legal documentation of de la Mare's manorial power, and forced him to agree a new document that accorded with the charter they had been offered by the king. This local rebellion was concluded with little bloodshed, with the only recorded fatality being the death of a man who was released when the peasants opened the Abbot's prison.

The comparative orderliness at St Albans contrasted with a violent rebellion against monastic power at Bury St Edmunds, in Suffolk. The revolt was led by John Wrawe, whose supporters executed several officials, including John of Cambridge, the Prior of Bury St Edmunds, who had fled from the Abbey when it was attacked on June 14. In the absence of the prior, the monks were forced to surrender their muniments, and issue a charter to the townspeople. A rising in Norfolk, led by Geoffrey Litster, who was proclaimed "King of the Commons", over-ran Norwich Castle. Cambridge University was attacked, many of its records were burnt, and a document was drawn up handing over its privileges to the people of Cambridge. Rebels plundered several of the villages that neighboured London – including Chiswick, Clapham, Croydon, Harrow, Hendon, and Twickenham. Winchester, the former capital city, was the scene of a rising by craftsmen against authority. Although London and the south east of England saw the most sustained rebellions, there were outbreaks as far north as Yorkshire.

King Richard had to act quickly if the government was to regain control. He therefore arranged another meeting with the peasants, which took place at Smithfield, to the north west of the Tower, on June 15, the day after the discussion at Mile End. Richard made staggering offers, promising the peasants their personal freedom from feudalism, abolition of the bishoprics and lordships, plus the confiscation by the state of all church land. Richard and his government did not intend to honour the pledges. William Walworth, the Mayor of London, rode up to Wat Tyler, as the latter addressed the king, called the rebel a "stinking wretch", and knocked him off his horse with a blow from a sword. One of the king's squires, Ralph Standish, completed the cold-blooded murder of Tyler, by stabbing the prostrate man in the stomach. The peasants held a strange reverence for Richard, and had stressed their loyalty to him, as opposed to the government and church leaders, throughout the revolt. The rebels apparently hoped that they could influence the young king to become a reformer, although some of them were developing the concept that popular revolt could actually replace the monarchy with a democratic government. Richard's combination of conciliation and determination continued to impress the peasants, and the meeting at Smithfield concluded without further violence. The Kentish peasants started to return to their homes, believing the government had accepted their demands, despite the murder of Tyler. Walworth returned to the City of London, and quickly assembled a force loyal to the government, which pursued the retreating peasants, and captured Jack Straw, who was executed.

Richard II and Sir Robert Tresilian, the Chief Justice, proceeded to tour counties which had seen the strongest rebellions. The king formally withdrew the terms offered to the peasants, claiming the agreements had been made under duress. Tresilian staged a series of trials, which led to the conviction and execution of hundreds of rebels. Although the government was unmerciful in suppressing the rebellion, it reluctantly abandoned the Poll Tax. Moving forward six centuries, the Community Charge was introduced by the Conservative government of Margaret Thatcher in 1990, with this flat rate charge on local government electors immediately becoming known as the Poll Tax. Comparisons were drawn with the past, and there was an anti-Poll Tax riot in London. Popular opposition contributed to the downfall of Thatcher. Her successor as Prime Minister, John Major, immediately planned a replacement for the Poll Tax. The Council Tax, arriving in 1993, was a fairer means to finance local government.

Richard II gradually took more power within government from 1381, and sole command, at the age of 22, in 1389. During the latter year, Richard had an Act of Parliament passed to ban football in England, due to concern that the game was distracting men from archery practice, with the latter being of national importance. Football was also banned, for this or other reasons, by Edward II (1314), Edward III (1349), Henry IV (1401), Edward IV (1477), and Henry VIII (1540). There were also laws against football in Scotland, from James I (1424) and James II (1457). Richard II's crushing of the peasants clouded his judgement, turning him into a despot, who made many enemies. He was forced to abdicate in 1399, being deposed by Henry, Second Duke of Lancaster, a son of John of Gaunt, who became Henry IV. An imprisoned Richard was probably starved to death in 1400.

The fifteenth century brought turbulent times for the monarchies of both England and Scotland. Henry IV (1399-1413) spent much of his reign defending against internal rebellions in England. Henry preferred to speak English instead of French, in contrast to each of the preceding kings since the Norman Conquest, more than three hundred years earlier. English had replaced French as the language used in the courts in 1362, as directed by the Pleading in English Act, to enable the majority of the population to understand the proceedings. From this point, English also started to be spoken in Parliament. Despite the precarious nature of his rule, Henry IV continued a tradition of Norman and Plantagenet kings, seeking to assert dominance over Wales and Scotland.

Owain Glyndwr, descended from the royal family of Powys, established a Welsh Parliament, and had himself crowned Tywysog Cymru (Prince of Wales) in 1404. Owain led a rebellion, aimed at securing Welsh independence, which stretched from 1400 to 1415. During the early years of the conflict, the Welsh received military support from France. The rebellion was defeated, but Owain Glyndwr has become a national hero, with much legend attached to his life. In 2000 – the year after the modern National Assembly for Wales was inaugurated – events were held to mark the sixth hundredth anniversary of Owain's rebellion. During 2004, an Internet poll aimed at ranking 100 Welsh Heroes placed Owain Glyndwr second, behind Aneurin Bevan, the Labour government minister who founded the National Health Service in 1948.

Henry IV invaded Scotland in 1400, marching to Edinburgh, but a siege of the castle there was abandoned. The Scottish king, Robert III (1390-1406), was the son of Robert II (1371-1390), and a great grandson of Robert Bruce. Robert II was the first of the Stewart dynasty to rule Scotland. The Stewarts, the spelling of whose name later changed to Stuart, were destined to be monarchs of Scotland through to 1714. In March 1406, Robert III attempted to send his young son and heir, James, to France, to protect him from rebellious members of the Scottish court. The ship in which James sailed was captured by pirates, and the boy was handed over to Henry IV. Robert III died in April 1406, and his son became King James I, but was destined to be a virtual prisoner of the English royal family for the next 18 years.

Henry IV was succeeded by his son, Henry V (1413-1422), who resumed war against France, dormant since 1389. Saint George's leadership was invoked by Henry V, in a speech prior to the English victory against the French at the Battle of Agincourt, in 1415. Later that year Henry Chichele, Archbishop of Canterbury, promoted Saint George's Day to the rank of a principal religious feast. In the twenty first century, Saint George's Day is recognised by the flying of flags from public buildings. Despite spirited campaigns from groups of patriotic citizens – and a Labour Party manifesto proposal in the 2017 and 2019 General Elections – April 23 is not a national holiday in England.

Following on from Agincourt, Henry V conquered Normandy, and other territory in France, with that country weakened by factional disputes during the reign of Charles VI, a man often troubled by psychosis. Provisions of the Treaty of Troyes, in 1420, included the marriage of Henry V to Catherine of Valois, daughter of Charles VI, with recognition of Henry as heir to the French throne. Henry V died in 1422, followed a few weeks later by Charles VI. Henry V was succeeded in England by his son Henry VI, an infant born the previous year. The latter was also proclaimed king of France – and eventually crowned at Notre-Dame, in Paris, during 1431. The claims of Henry VI in France were challenged by a son of Charles VI, who was crowned as Charles VII at Reims in 1429 – as his military position improved, inspired by spiritual intervention from Joan of Arc. During 1421, James I of Scotland, whose position as a captive was becoming flexible, campaigned with Henry V in France. James married Joan Beaufort, a granddaughter of John of Gaunt, in 1424. He was now released by the government of Henry VI, upon payment of a ransom, and returned to Scotland. James remained king until 1437, when he was assassinated by disaffected nobles, and succeeded by his son James II, who was aged six. The Hundred Years War lasted until 1453, with Charles VII reversing the victories of Henry V, and regaining territory. As the war ended, Henry VI suffered a mental breakdown, and English claims to a joint monarchy, also covering France, were abandoned. A formal peace treaty did not follow until 1475, being agreed by the respective monarchs at that time, Edward IV and Louis XI.

The Wars of the Roses were fought, at intervals across thirty years, between the Lancastrian and Yorkist branches of the Plantagenet dynasty. Conflict stemmed from the weak rule of the Lancastrian Henry VI, and rebellion, led by Richard, Third Duke of York. Richard was descended in the male line from Edmund of Langley, First Duke of York, a son of Edward III. Richard also had a descent – via his mother, Anne Mortimer – from Lionel of Antwerp, First Duke of Clarence, another of Edward III's sons. The Yorkists won the first battle of the war, at St Albans, in 1455. The Lancastrians managed to seal an alliance with James II of Scotland. James achieved success in quelling domestic rebellion with use of the cannon, a weapon new to Scotland, which he had imported from the Low Countries, home of his wife, Mary of Guelders. In 1460, James, besieging Roxburgh Castle – north of the border with England – in aid of Henry VI, fired a cannon to celebrate the arrival of Mary, but he was fatally wounded by an explosion. The siege continued, and the royal army captured the castle, which was then destroyed, upon an order by Mary. The late king's son became James III, at the age of eight – a third successive minority monarch of Scotland.

Henry VI of England was deposed in 1461 by Edward IV, a son of Richard, Third Duke of York, whereupon Henry took refuge in Scotland. Henry was restored as king in 1470, but in the following year was again removed by Edward, with the Yorkists winning the Battle of

Tewkesbury. Henry was murdered, probably upon the orders of Edward, the latter of whom reigned until his own death, in 1483. During 1474, a betrothal was agreed for Cecily, a daughter of Edward IV, and James, son of James III of Scotland – at a time when both Cecily and the younger James were infants. The planned marriage did not actually happen, but the relevant agreement is of note, as it mentioned "this Nobill Isle, callit Gret Britanee". This is the earliest known official reference to the idea of Great Britain. In 1483, Edward IV was succeeded by his son Edward V, aged 12, who was in turn rapidly replaced by Richard III, a brother of Edward IV. Edward V and his brother, Richard, were held captive in the Tower of London by Richard III – their uncle. The two boys disappeared, apparently being murdered, and are known to history as "the Princes in the Tower".

The Wars of the Roses ended with the Battle of Bosworth, on August 22 1485, as Henry Tudor, a Lancastrian, and great great grandson of John of Gaunt, defeated Richard III, who was killed in the fighting. After an exile in France, avoiding possible capture by the Yorkists, Henry Tudor had only recently returned to Britain, landing with an army at Pembrokeshire, in Wales. Henry had been born at Pembroke Castle, in 1457, and gained Welsh support for his campaign, with the Tudors being descended from the monarchs of Deheubarth. The body of Richard III was hastily buried in a church, subsequently demolished in the dissolution of the monasteries, under Henry VIII. In 2012 a search for the body of Richard was successful, with his remains being found under a car park in Leicester. Richard III was subsequently re-buried at Leicester Cathedral, in 2015.

7 Early Modern Britain

The year 1485 is taken to be the end of the Middle Ages, and start of the Early Modern era, in the history of England and, by extension, Britain. Henry Tudor became King Henry VII, upon his victory at Bosworth, establishing the Tudor dynasty in England. Henry rapidly asserted his authority, defeating plots aimed at placing a Yorkist, or even a non-royal "pretender", on the throne. In 1486 Henry married Elizabeth of York, a daughter of Edward IV, and introduced the Tudor Rose emblem, combining the red rose of Lancaster with the white rose of York, in an act of reconciliation. In Scotland, the rule of James III was being challenged, and he was killed in 1488 by rebels, backed by his son, who now became James IV, at the age of 15. In 1502, Henry VII and James IV agreed the Treaty of Perpetual Peace, aimed at ending the intermittent warfare between England and Scotland, fought since the army of the former invaded the latter in 1296. The treaty led to Margaret Tudor, a daughter of Henry, marrying James in 1503 – this was 29 years after his betrothal to Cecily of York. Despite the Stuarts being the weaker party compared to the Tudors, this inter-marriage between the two families led to the Scottish dynasty inheriting the English crown a century later, following which they began to shape a new state of Great Britain.

Henry VII died in 1509, being succeeded by a son, Henry VIII. The young and handsome prince became a prematurely aged monster, as Henry VIII's political machinations took him through marriage to a series of six wives, two of whom, Anne Boleyn and Catherine Howard, were first cousins, and both beheaded. Favourite ministers also came and went – with Henry ordering the executions of Thomas Wolsey, Thomas More, and Thomas Cromwell. Breaking the supposed Perpetual Peace, James IV led an attempted Scottish invasion of England in 1513, at a time when Henry VIII was campaigning in France. James IV now died at the Battle of Flodden, and remains the last British monarch to be killed in battle. Henry VIII had appointed Catherine of Aragon, his first wife, regent during this absence, with the title "Governor of the Realm and Captain General", and she oversaw the English military defence against the Scots.

In order to obtain a divorce from Catherine of Aragon, Henry VIII carried out a break with the Roman Catholic church. Besides defying the Papacy, Henry's action put him in opposition to Charles V, the Holy Roman Emperor, who was also king of Spain, and a nephew of Catherine. Charles was the most powerful ruler in Europe at this time, with control of territory approaching that of Charlemagne, seven centuries earlier. Henry appointed himself Supreme Head of the new Church of England in 1534, as he initiated the English Reformation.

There was widespread plunder of religious houses in this country. Thomas Wriothesley, later created the first Earl of Southampton, acted as one of the king's religious commissioners. During the early hours of September 21 1538, Wriothesley led an attack on Winchester Cathedral, which included the destruction of Saint Swithin's Shrine. Parish Registers were introduced, in 1538, by an English government wishing more information about the population. Each church in the Church of England was required to record baptisms, marriages, and burials. Wales was legally united with England, by legislation initiated by Henry VIII's government in 1536 and 1543. Henry was also recognised as king of Ireland, persuading that nation's Parliament to pass the Crown of Ireland Act in 1542. This legislation, which became known among Irish nationalists as the Act of Annexation, was part of a long-running English attempt to establish rule as a conquering power.

Back in England, the despotic Statute of Proclamations, of 1539, gave the crown the right to issue legislation without reference to Parliament. In modern times, provisions in Acts of Parliament allowing government ministers to amend, or repeal, an Act through secondary legislation – which is not subject to full Parliamentary scrutiny – have become known as "Henry VIII powers". Nearly five centuries after Henry's break with the Roman Catholic Church, the aftermath of the European Union referendum of 2016 saw a Conservative government introduce sweeping "Henry VIII powers", in their Brexit legislation, as Britain broke from the Treaty of Rome, and other EU rules.

The will of Henry VIII, who died in 1547, made his son, Edward, successor to the throne, followed by Mary and Elizabeth, the daughters of Catherine of Aragon and Anne Boleyn respectively. If his three children died without heirs, Henry directed the throne should transfer to the family of his sister Mary. This Mary had died in 1533, and her immediate heir was now a daughter, Frances Brandon. Jane Grey, the oldest daughter of Frances, plus her husband Henry Grey, Marquess of Dorset, was born in 1537 – a great niece of Henry VIII. With Edward VI being only nine years old, a royal council governed in his name. Initially the leading figure was Edward Seymour, Duke of Somerset, a brother of Jane Seymour, Henry VIII's third wife, who had died, as a result of natal complications, a few days after the future Edward VI's birth. Thomas Seymour, another brother, was a member of the council, and Lord High Admiral. In 1549, Edward Seymour was disgraced, and John Dudley ousted him as leader of the council. Edward Seymour was subsequently executed in 1552.

Edward VI and John Dudley, created Duke of Northumberland in 1551, were staunch Protestants, seeking religious development of the English Reformation, which Henry VIII instigated for political motives.

Edward disliked his sister Mary, a fervent Roman Catholic, and was uncertain about the strength of Elizabeth's Protestant intentions. During 1553, Northumberland hatched a plan to make Jane Grey the queen, and control her, as the wife of his son Guilford. Northumberland arranged the marriage with Jane's parents, who abandoned a betrothal of Jane to Edward Seymour, Lord Hertford, a son of the late Duke of Somerset. Jane married Guilford Dudley, at the Strand in London, on May 21, and was ill for several weeks following the wedding, apparently due to stress caused by an unwelcome union. Edward, suffering from tuberculosis, exacerbated by other ailments, signed a Device of Succession, which named Jane as heir to the throne. Edward died on July 6 and, three days later, members of the late king's council informed Jane that she was now queen. Jane replied "The crown is not my right, and pleaseth me not, the Lady Mary is the rightful heir", but was persuaded to accept a dubious duty.

Jane is remembered as "the Nine Days Queen", with her reign being the shortest tenure of an English sovereign. Upon being publicly proclaimed monarch, on July 10, Jane took up residence in the royal apartment at the Tower of London, along with Guilford Dudley. Like her predecessor, Matilda, in the twelfth century, Jane faced a rival claimant for the throne. Mary gained considerable support among the nobility, as the legal heir of Henry VIII. The royal council buckled in the face of Mary's determination, and rushed to declare loyalty, in a cynical attempt to save their influence. The council issued the proclamation of Mary as monarch on July 19, abruptly ending the reign of Queen Jane. Henry Grey left Jane in the Tower of London, to become a prisoner of the new royal government.

Mary had Northumberland executed, while Jane was informed the new monarch planned to have her convicted of treason, but a pardon and freedom would follow. Mary's position as queen was recognised with a coronation, at Westminster Abbey, on October 1. Jane and Guilford Dudley were tried at the Guildhall, in the City of London, on November 14, pleaded guilty to treason, and sentenced to death. Mary planned to marry Philip, the son of Charles V, and heir to the Spanish throne, to signal the re-establishment of Catholicism. This prompted Protestant rebellions, at several locations, at the beginning of 1554. The most serious uprising emanated from Kent, led by Thomas Wyatt, with support from Henry Grey. Wyatt and the rebels marched on London, but were defeated. Upon advice from members of the royal council, who had forced an unwilling Jane to become monarch a few months earlier, Mary reluctantly concluded that Jane and Guilford should be executed.

Jane faced execution, on February 12, with amazing dignity and courage, as a 16 year old girl wrongly condemned to death, in punishment for the failed conspiracies of others. Jane's body, and that of Guilford, was buried in the chapel of St Peter ad Vincula, at the Tower of London. Jane was buried beside Anne Boleyn and Catherine Howard. The Duke of Northumberland had been buried there, as had the Duke of Somerset before him. Eleven days after Jane was executed, her father was beheaded, and his body was also buried in the chapel. The life, and death, of Jane is one of the most poignant events in the story of the English monarchy.

Queen Mary tried to turn the clock back to Catholicism, with three hundred Protestants being executed as heretics – nearly all of them were burnt to death – but the savage policy of "Bloody Mary" did not work. Her marriage to Philip of Spain, in July 1554, and wish to have him recognised as king of England, proved unpopular. Mary became queen consort of Naples upon the marriage, and also took this title in respect of Spain, when her husband became King Philip II of that country in 1556, upon the abdication of his father, Charles. Spain was becoming one of the wealthiest states in Europe, as colonisation of the Americas, begun by Christopher Columbus in 1492, brought massive amounts of gold and silver, seized from the native peoples of the New World. Mary died on November 17 1558, being succeeded by her half-sister, Elizabeth.

Queen Elizabeth was destined to reign for nearly 45 years, through to 1603, and prove a great success, but for much of this time there was uncertainty. The decision not to marry left her without an heir. In early 1559, only a few weeks after the death of Mary, the widowed Philip of Spain unsuccessfully suggested marriage to Elizabeth. Through the 1560s and 1570s, the queen entertained courtship from a series of foreign royals. The last of these was Francis Duke of Anjou, a Catholic who had intrigued with Protestants against his brother, Henry III of France. When marriage negotiations began in 1579, Elizabeth was aged 46, and therefore probably beyond child-bearing, while Francis was only 24. She broke off their possible union two years later.

Mary Queen of Scots (granddaughter of James IV and Margaret Tudor), was forced to abdicate in 1567, as members of the nobility rebelled. She had acceded to the throne, aged just six days old, on the death of her father, James V, in 1542. Mary was replaced as monarch by her son, James VI, who was little more than a year old at the time. Imprisoned in Scotland, Mary managed to escape in 1568, fleeing to England, only to be incarcerated there. Mary spent 19 years in captivity in England, during which time she was a focus of Catholic opposition to Elizabeth. This included the Rising of the North, in 1569, led by nobles in northern England. In 1583, the Throckmorton Plot, led by Sir Francis Throckmorton, sought to make Mary the queen of England, with support from Catholics in Spain and France. The plan was discovered, and

Throckmorton was executed the following year. The Babington Plot of 1586, led by Anthony Babington and John Ballard, English Catholics, also aimed at the replacement of Elizabeth by Mary. The plan was communicated to Mary, who endorsed it. This led to Elizabeth having her rival tried, and convicted of treason, following which Mary was executed in 1587.

The Dutch Republic, a Protestant state, declared independence from Spanish rule of the Netherlands, during 1581. The Dutch revolt was led by William of Orange, a man who would be assassinated in 1584. Elizabeth agreed the Treaty of Nonsuch, with the Dutch, in 1585, pledging military assistance. The alliance was signed at Nonsuch Palace, in Surrey, the building of which had been started by Henry VIII. English support for the Dutch led to an intermittent Anglo-Spanish War, which lasted until 1604. The Spanish Armada, a fleet of 130 ships, attempted an invasion of England in 1588, but this was thwarted during battles in the English Channel. The Spanish Armada actually set sail from Lisbon, in Portugal, with Philip II having been king of both countries since 1580 – Portugal would become independent again in 1640. Part of the reason for Spain launching the attack was a wish to block English support for the Dutch. The key encounter was the Battle of Gravelines, a port in the Netherlands, fought on August 8. The Armada attempted to meet up with the Spanish army active in the Netherlands, but were prevented from doing this, as the English and Dutch navies combined to defeat them. On the day of the battle, an English army, stationed at West Tilbury, in Essex, prepared to defend against a possible Spanish attack on the Thames Estuary. They were visited by Elizabeth, and she addressed them in a famous speech the next day – before news of the naval victory had reached her:

Let tyrants fear. I have always so behaved myself that, under God, I have placed my chiefest strength and safeguard in the loyal hearts and goodwill of my subjects. And, therefore, I am come amongst you as you see at this time, not for my recreation and disport, but being resolved, in the midst and heat of battle, to live or die amongst you all. To lay down for my God, and for my kingdoms, and for my people, my honour and my blood even in the dust. I know I have the body of a weak and feeble woman, but I have the heart and stomach of a king – and of a king of England too.

Within a few days, struggling due to lack of supplies, plus strong winds off the east coast of England, the Spanish Armada abandoned the planned invasion. After a long journey around the coast of Scotland, many vessels were shipwrecked to the west of Ireland, and only half of the original fleet arrived back in Spain.

When Elizabeth died, centuries of rivalry between the monarchies of England and Scotland ended. The crowns were united, in the person of James Stuart, son of Mary Queen of Scots. He reigned from 1567 to 1625 as James VI of Scotland, and from 1603 to 1625 as James I of England plus Wales. The body of Elizabeth was placed in a tomb, located at Westminster Abbey, which already held the remains of Mary Tudor. King James arranged for a Latin inscription to be placed on the tomb, with an English translation being "Consorts in realm and tomb, here we sleep, Elizabeth and Mary, sisters, in hope of resurrection".

During the final years of what we now call the Elizabethan era, William Shakespeare emerged as a leading playwright, with a series of popular works staged in London. He has retained a massive reputation through to the present day, generally being acclaimed as Britain's greatest ever writer. Shakespeare was born in 1564, with the exact date traditionally being regarded as April 23, St George's Day, and he definitely died on that date in 1616. He wrote plays on diverse subjects, including "histories", based to a greater or lesser extent on facts. Shakespeare was the author of plays about eight historic kings of England, stretching in actual chronology from *The Life and Death of King John* to *Henry VIII*, besides the legendary *King Lear* and *Cymbeline*. In *The Life and Death of King Richard the Second*, Shakespeare imagines a speech by John of Gaunt, who laments the decline of the nation during the rule of Richard. In the course of the oration, the country is referred to as "This Sceptered Isle", followed by "This precious stone set in the silver sea" and also "This blessed plot, this earth, this realm, this England". There was also *The Tragedy of Macbeth*, Shakespeare's "Scottish Play", long-reputed in theatrical circles to be unlucky. Scholars have concluded that *Macbeth* was probably written in 1606, with allusions in the text being taken as celebration of the accession of King James to the English throne. Perhaps an unluckier play was Shakespeare's *Henry VIII*, with the misfiring of a cannon, during a performance in 1613, causing the Globe Theatre, at Southwark in London, to be destroyed by flames. The theatre was rebuilt the following year, but closed down by Puritans in 1642, and subsequently demolished. A modern reconstruction of the theatre, called Shakespeare's Globe, opened in 1997, with a production of *Henry V*, reputedly the first play performed at the original Globe, when it was opened by Shakespeare and his associates, in 1599.

In 1605 the Gunpowder Plot was launched by a group of Catholics, who sought to kill the Protestant King James, at the State Opening of

Parliament, on November 5. This was thwarted, as Guy Fawkes was found preparing to use gunpowder, to cause an explosion, on the evening of November 4. The main organiser was Robert Catesby, a son of Anne Throckmorton, the latter of whom was a cousin of Sir Francis Throckmorton, executed for his role in the 1583 intrigue against Queen Elizabeth. Catesby was shot dead on November 8 1605, as a force led by Sir Richard Walsh, the Sheriff of Worcestershire, surrounded some of the conspirators at Holbeche House, in Staffordshire. Fawkes and other participants in the Gunpowder Plot were put on trial, at Westminster Hall, during 1606, convicted, and executed. To this day, their defeat is commemorated on November 5, Bonfire Night, with effigies of Guy Fawkes being burnt.

James issued a proclamation, styling himself "King of Great Brittaine, France, and Ireland", in 1604. Two years later, James unveiled a flag, uniting those of England and Scotland, to represent "this Isle and Kingdome of Great Britaine" – with the spelling edging closer to the current Britain. There was not a Welsh element in the flag, a reflection of Wales having been legally united with England by Henry VIII. James believed in the "divine right of kings", a theory that monarchs rule due to the will of God, and should not be subject to control by fellow human beings. James did not push this doctrine in practice, but his son, Charles I (1625-1649), attempted autocratic rule, which led to clashes with Parliament, and the English Civil War, fought at intervals between 1642 and 1651. The Parliamentary side improved its strength with the formation of the New Model Army, in 1645, with Oliver Cromwell, an MP, having a leading role. There was much political discussion among this army, and various manifestos were issued, most notably a series entitled *An Agreement of the People*. During 1647, the Putney Debates (held at Putney, then a town in Surrey, now a suburb of London) considered plans for a written constitution. Thomas Rainsborough, an MP and prominent member of the Levellers, a radical group, argued for an extension of the franchise to all men. Rainsborough was recorded as saying:

For really I think that the poorest hee that is in England hath a life to live, as the greatest hee; and therefore truly, Sr, I think it clear, that every Man that is to live under a Government ought first by his own Consent to put himself under that Government; and I do think that the poorest man in England is not at all bound in a strict sense to that Government that he hath not had a voice to put himself under.

In recent times, the seventeenth century radical name has been recalled by the Levellers, a folk rock music band, active since their foundation in

1988. The Diggers, a similar Civil War group, advocated public health insurance, three hundred years prior to the formation of the National Health Service in 1948.

After a series of military defeats were inflicted upon the Royalist army, King Charles was deposed by Parliament, tried at Westminster Hall, and beheaded in 1649. England became a republic, and Puritan influence within the regime of Oliver Cromwell famously suppressed the celebration of Christmas. More importantly, religious bigotry against Catholics led to the English republic carrying out a brutal military campaign in Ireland, which included the killing of civilians. With the independence of Scotland also crushed, Cromwell was declared "Lord Protector of the Commonwealth of England, Scotland and Ireland" in 1653. The phrase comes from the Instrument of Government, passed by the English Parliament, as a written constitution for Britain. The idea was updated by the Humble Petition and Advice in 1657, but subsequent restoration of the monarchy ended this development. When Oliver Cromwell died in 1658, his role as head of the republic was incongruously inherited by a son, Richard. Thereafter the republic declined, with Richard Cromwell a far less effective figure than his father. The actions of Oliver Cromwell have, to an extent, undermined campaigns for a new republic, in the period of over three centuries since that era.

The growing unpopularity of the republic led Parliament to recall the monarchy. In May 1660, an English expedition sailed to the Netherlands, and returned Charles, son of the late king, from exile. Upon his arrival in England, the son was proclaimed King Charles II. The group accompanying Charles on his voyage included Samuel Pepys, destined to become known as the author of Britain's most celebrated diary. During his lifetime, Pepys' reputation stemmed from work as a navy administrator, who became a Member of Parliament. During the 1660s Pepys kept a private diary, as a virtually daily record that was to stretch to more than a million words. Eventual publication revealed Pepys as an exceptionally skilled recorder of political events – as both witness and participant. He was also an engaging chronicler of everyday life. Pepys started to write a diary, using shorthand, on the first day of 1660, at the age of 26. Pepys kept a detailed account of his activities, and thoughts, in the journal – this being the word that he used. His work for the navy was explained at length, as public service was combined with attendant opportunities for private enterprise, enabling Pepys to accumulate a personal fortune. Samuel's domestic routines with his wife, Elizabeth St Michel, featured in the diary, and trouble with servants was a recurring theme. He obviously enjoyed socialising with family and friends, as drinking, eating, and visits to the theatre were chronicled, along with progress in learning to sing and play musical instruments. Pepys was a womaniser, who was frequently unfaithful to Elizabeth, and recorded his sexual liaisons with a series of women in the diary. Throughout the diary Pepys wrote extensively, and repetitively, about matters such as the time he got up in the morning, his finances, the weather, and the food that he ate. Pepys regularly ended entries by noting that he ate supper and went to bed.

Pepys wrote a lot about the Great Plague, a tragedy estimated to have claimed the lives of as many as 100,000 people in London, during 1665 and 1666. In the latter year, the Great Fire of London raged for four days and, on September 4, Pepys noted that "Pauls is burned, and all Cheapside", the former of these being the old St Paul's Cathedral. This cathedral had been built by the Normans to replace the Church of St Paul the Apostle, which had been wrecked by fire in 1087. The tomb of Ethelred "the Unready", which had escaped the effects of the blaze in 1087, was lost in the fire of 1666. The current St Paul's Cathedral was constructed between 1675 and 1710. Although St Paul's has not staged as many state occasions as Westminster Abbey, the former was the venue for the marriage of Prince Charles and Diana Spencer in 1981. This was the first royal wedding at the site since Prince Arthur, son of Henry VII, married Catherine of Aragon, at the old St Paul church, in 1501.

The catastrophes of plague and fire in London coincided with national crisis, stemming from the Second Anglo-Dutch War of 1665 to 1667 – this being one of four such conflicts, at intervals between 1652 and 1784. The war against the Netherlands revolved around naval battles, including an audacious Dutch raid along the River Thames in 1667, and Pepys had an important administrative role. Pepys ceased writing the diary on May 31 1669, fearing for his eyesight. He had been experiencing pains in his eyes for five years, and these were to continue for the remainder of his life, but Pepys' worry that he would go blind proved unfounded. More importantly, an unexpected tragedy struck later in 1669, as Elizabeth died on November 10, aged just 29, from the effects of a fever caught during an extended holiday with Samuel in the Netherlands, Flanders, and France.

The restored monarchy was plunged into a period of uncertainty, in the form of the Exclusion Crisis. This stemmed from an attempt by Protestants in Parliament to exclude James, the Catholic brother of Charles II, from the succession. The Parliamentarians pushing for Exclusion, a campaign they started in 1678, were dubbed Whigs by their opponents. This referred back to the Whiggamores, a Presbyterian group active during the Civil War. The Whigs in turn started, in 1681, to call the supporters of James by the name Tory. A Tory was originally an Irish outlaw. The Whigs and Tories both accepted their critical nicknames as a badge of honour, and many members of Parliament quickly became loyal to one of these embryo political parties.

Charles II died in 1685, being succeeded by James II, whose attempt to restore Catholicism to Britain led to his downfall. In 1688, twenty eight years after Charles II had returned from the Netherlands, his nephew William of Orange, a Dutchman married to Mary, a daughter of James II, invaded England. William and his forces arrived at Brixham, a few miles away from Totnes in Devon – the legendary landing place of Brutus – on November 5, which was coincidentally the anniversary of the date planned for the assassination of James I in 1605. The advance of William of Orange – a great grandson of the William who led the Dutch to independence – prompted James II to flee to France, and ushered in the supposed Glorious Revolution of 1688. For the native ruling class, William of Orange was a welcome liberator of England, in contrast to William the Conqueror. Parliament formally concluded that James had abdicated, following which William III and Mary II took the throne as joint monarchs, on February 13 1689. The process was followed by the Bill of Rights, an Act of the English and Welsh Parliament. This law – along with the equivalent Claim of Right Act passed in Scotland – defined the respective roles of the monarch and Parliament, while also setting out rights for the citizens of Britain. Supporters of the legislation have long hailed this as a cornerstone of British freedom, similar to Magna Carta, but it was limited. The right to vote in Parliamentary Elections was still restricted to a small minority of men, who owned property.

Samuel Pepys was falsely suspected of supporting attempts by James II to regain power, being imprisoned in 1689, and again the following year. During retirement, Pepys' main enthusiasm was the massive expansion, and cataloguing, of his library, with assistance from his nephew, John Jackson, to whom it was bequeathed. Pepys instructed that, upon the death of Jackson, the collection would be transferred to Magdalene College at Cambridge University – where Pepys had been a student as a youth – to be preserved "for the benefit of posterity". Samuel Pepys moved from London to Clapham (at that time a small town beyond the boundaries of the capital city) in 1701, and it was at Clapham that he died, on May 26 1703, aged 70. More than a century passed before the shorthand diary was transcribed, and a selection, edited by Lord Braybrooke, was published in 1825 by Henry Colburn (the man who issued Benjamin Disraeli's debut novel, *Vivian Grey*, to a rather baffled readership the following year).

One result of the arrival of William of Orange in England was that the country joined the Netherlands, in an international coalition, fighting against France, in 1689 – a conflict now known as the Nine Years War, which lasted from 1688 to 1697. The Bank of England was formed in 1694, initially as a means to finance an improved navy. The bank was set up as a private organisation, by wealthy individuals, and lent money to the government, besides being authorised to issue bank notes. This borrowing by William III's government was the start of the National Debt and, in the first few decades, a high proportion of this was owed to Dutchmen. The Bank of England remained a source of private profit for 252 years, until it was nationalised, for the benefit of the British people, by a Labour government in 1946.

William and Mary were childless and, following the death of Mary in 1694, the Act of Settlement 1701 set out a Protestant succession to the throne, excluding many Catholic claimants. William III died in 1702, and the crown passed to Queen Anne, a sister of Mary II. The Jacobite supporters, and descendants, of James II, who died in 1701, made consistent efforts to restore a Catholic monarchy. A major rebellion led by a grandson of James, namely Charles Stuart (also known as Bonnie Prince Charlie), was defeated at the Battle of Culloden in 1746. The Jacobites eventually dropped their claim to the British throne in 1807. During Anne's reign, an Act of Union was passed by the Parliament of England and Wales in 1706, and mirrored by the legislature of Scotland the following year, formally uniting these nations on May 1 1707. Over a century after the Stuarts founded a joint monarchy, two separate Parliaments merged into a single replacement, based in London. The distant dawn of Roman Britannia had been echoed by the establishment of Great Britain.

8 The Age of Empire

The state of Great Britain, hesitantly constructed during the Stuart era, rapidly gained strength thereafter, as the centre of a vast empire. The scale, and power, of the British Empire would exceed that of the Romans, or Charlemagne, or indeed any other imperial force in world history. British nationalists, past and present, have wished to forget that a family from Germany, the Hanoverians, occupied the British throne for nearly two centuries, at the height of this power. The Protestant Stuart line died with Queen Anne, and the British crown transferred to her second cousin, George I, who was already the ruler of Hanover. With four successive kings being named George, historians refer to the period 1714 to 1820 as the Georgian Era. In view of English royalty's promotion of the cult of Saint George, it is surprising that only six of the nation's kings have borne the name George – with each of these having ruled in the last three hundred years, rather than the Middle Ages. George I was born at Hanover, on May 28 1660 – coincidentally the day before Charles II became king, upon the restoration of the monarchy. George had virtually no prospect of becoming king of England, until the Act of Settlement in 1701, whereupon the Hanoverian royals began to prepare for possible succession. The future George II, born in Hanover during 1683, became a naturalised Briton in 1705.

Following upheavals of civil war, republic, and restoration, in the seventeenth century, the newly united Britain slowly moved towards rule by a constitutional monarchy – without a written constitution – from 1707. The office of Prime Minister was effectively established during the reign of George I, by Robert Walpole, a Whig politician. Walpole led the government from 1721 until 1742, with most of this tenure serving George II, a son of George I, who reigned from 1727 until 1760, and unfortunately died of a heart attack, while sat on a lavatory. Robert Walpole was born in 1676, being the son of Colonel Robert Walpole, who was MP from 1689 to 1700 for Castle Rising, in Norfolk. The younger Robert was elected to Parliament for Castle Rising in 1701, before moving to King's Lynn, also in Norfolk, the following year. During 1712, Walpole was found guilty of corruption, expelled from Parliament, and imprisoned in the Tower of London, but he was re-elected in 1713. He was the father of Horace Walpole, who invented the Gothic novel, with the self-published *The Castle of Otranto* in 1764. Horace was also an MP from 1741 to 1768, successively representing Callington, in Cornwall (a place he never visited), Castle Rising, and King's Lynn.

From the time of the Norman Conquest, military rivalry of England – and subsequently Britain – with France was a consistent theme in our history for several centuries. During the eighteenth and nineteenth centuries, with the British monarchs being from a German dynasty, there was a resumption of the idealised Anglo-Saxon heritage. This was also the dawn of *Rule, Britannia!*, a patriotic – or belligerent – song, reflecting a strengthened navy, which led to increased military, and economic, power for the British state. With lyrics by James Thomson, set to music by Thomas Arne, *Rule, Britannia!* first appeared in *Alfred*, a play celebrating the heroic struggle of that king against the Vikings. The play was commissioned by Frederick Louis, Prince of Wales, son of George II and father of George III, being performed in 1740 at his home, Cliveden, in Buckinghamshire. In later years, Cliveden would become the seat of the Astor family, and a setting for events in the Profumo Scandal of the early 1960s. The Astors gifted the estate to the National Trust, and the grounds are open to the public, but the actual house has been leased to private companies, as a luxury hotel, since 1985.

Britain fought alongside Germans in the Seven Years War, which lasted from 1756 to 1763. One side was led by Britain, with support from Hanover, Prussia, and other German states. The adversary was led by France, allied with the Austrian Empire, Russia, and Spain. The Seven Years War stretched across several continents, and its scale has led some historians to refer to it as World War Zero, due to it anticipating the later World War One.

George III, born in London during 1738, never visited Germany, despite also being the ruler of Hanover throughout his reign as king of Britain. After a happy childhood, during which he developed a particular interest in science, the adult George plunged into possible scandal. He had a relationship with Hannah Lightfoot, a young woman from Wapping who was a commoner, with her father being a humble shoemaker. It was later alleged that George secretly married Hannah, in 1759, with the couple having three children together. Documentation regarding the matter has been kept secret in the royal archives since 1866, prompting claims of an official cover-up, but this may simply be cobblers.

George became king on October 25 1760, at the age of 22, and was destined to reign for more than 59 years, until his death in 1820, but for the last nine years of this period George's position was only nominal. George married Charlotte of Mecklenburg-Strelitz, a German princess, on September 8 1761. Fourteen days later George was crowned at Westminster Abbey, with the queen at his side. During the ceremony a jewel fell out of the crown, an incident which was later taken to be an omen for the loss of Britain's American colonies. George and Charlotte made a happy couple, who were to have 15 children. George had difficult relations with his eldest son, also named George.

George III faced outspoken criticism during the early years of his reign from John Wilkes, a Member of Parliament who combined advocacy of free speech with a scandalous private life. The main event of George's reign was the American war of 1775 to 1783. Britain's defeat, and the American Declaration of Independence in 1776, left George with a poor reputation, both in his lifetime and subsequently. He survived two of the rare assassination attempts against a British monarch – the actions of the assailants, Margaret Nicholson (1786) and James Hadfield (1800), were attributed to insanity. The sovereign retained his early interest in learning, and even published articles on agriculture, using the pseudonym Ralph Robinson, which led to him being derided as "Farmer George" by some critics.

The king experienced a severe breakdown, which began with "the Cheltenham episode", as George was laid low in June 1788, during a visit to Cheltenham. As George explained in a letter to William Pitt the Younger, the ailment was "a pretty smart bilious attack". The king suffered pain in his stomach and bowels, accompanied by violent diarrhoea. George quickly recovered from this attack, but in August fell ill with influenza. On October 17 there was a recurrence of George's stomach ailment, plus pain in his legs. This was rapidly followed by other symptoms, and by the end of the month George was racked with both physical and mental agony. During November, he was moved from Windsor to Kew, where the royal physicians, who had been unable to tackle the mystery ailment, were joined by Francis Willis. A Regency Bill was introduced in Parliament, aimed at making the Prince of Wales regent for his father, but the king's recovery during the early part of 1789, as he benefitted from treatment initiated by Willis, put an end to the scheme. George III enjoyed a spell of convalescence at Weymouth, and was soon back in command of the state.

The true nature of George III's illness eluded his doctors. In the 1930s, he was posthumously diagnosed as having suffered from porphyria, a hereditary metabolic condition, which affects the blood and nervous system. The origin has been traced back to Charles VI of France, the father of Catherine of Valois, the latter of whom was the wife of Henry V. Catherine's subsequent relationship with Owen Tudor made her an ancestor of the Tudor monarchs, and led to porphyria continuing to afflict the English royal family after the extinction of Henry V's line. Catherine's tomb was damaged during the reign of Henry VII, her grandson, and her body became a gruesome tourist attraction. Catherine was not properly re-buried until 1878, on the orders of Queen Victoria.

The Madness of King George, a film released in 1994, is a brilliant dramatisation of the episode of ill health that afflicted the monarch during 1788 and 1789. The ailment is not stated until a note appears, in the final credits, mentioning porphyria. More than two hundred years after the events it covered, the film succeeded in portraying George III as a remarkable, and troubled, human being, surrounded by both family and political intrigue. The cinema piece was based on the 1991 play *The Madness of George III* by Alan Bennett. A moving portrayal of George's illness is combined with subtle comedy. Nigel Hawthorne starred as George III, while Helen Mirren played Queen Charlotte. Mirren had previously played Morganna in *Excalibur* (a 1981 re-working of the Arthurian legends), and would subsequently portray Elizabeth II in *The Queen* (2006).

Early in the film, as George's behaviour becomes erratic, he conducts an orchestra in a performance of George Friedrich Handel's *Water Music* – a piece written for George I, with the composer being one of that monarch's courtiers. Perhaps the best comedy arrives as George, during the recovery from illness, leads a group reading from Shakespeare's *King Lear*, an earlier tale of a monarch at the edge of sanity. George delivers lines from the play with great enthusiasm, while others show an embarrassed reticence. The final minutes depict George, and the royal family, celebrating his return to good health, in a ceremony at St Paul's Cathedral. This sequence is a brilliant satire on the House of Windsor, as George III suggests "we must try to be more of a family", while the Prince of Wales laments his lack of a clear role, just as the then holder of that title, Charles, was known to do. *The Madness of King George* arrived just two years after Elizabeth II suffered what she called the "annus horribilis" of 1992, when the separation of Prince Charles from Diana Spencer was followed by a severe fire at Windsor Castle. The plot was destined to thicken, with more medical scholarship on the subject of George's illness. Modern interpretations suggest he may have been suffering from Bipolar Disorder, rather than Porphyria. This research has been facilitated by the opening up of George III's papers, by the Royal Archives, to public scrutiny in recent years – followed by a digitised mass of this material being placed on the Internet in 2017.

In 1800 the government of William Pitt the Younger – who had been Prime Minister since taking office in 1783, at the age of just 24 – passed the Act of Union, which formally united Britain with Ireland on January 1 1801. On that date, the Union Flag was introduced, combining the 1606 British flag with Saint Patrick's Saltire, representing Ireland – Wales was still not directly included. The Parliament of Ireland, founded in 1297, was abolished. George III now renounced his theoretical claim to be king of France – the title having been declared by all English monarchs since it was asserted by Edward III, in 1340, during the Hundred Years War. On the other hand, a war against France began in 1793, four years after the start of the French Revolution. The war featured two famous British victories, led by Horatio Nelson at Trafalgar in 1805, and Arthur Wellesley, Duke of Wellington, at Waterloo in 1815. The first battle was a naval engagement, fought off Cape Trafalgar, in Spain, while the latter was a land encounter, near the town of Waterloo, now in Belgium. Within a few decades, their names were recalled at two sites in the capital of the United Kingdom, Trafalgar Square and London Waterloo railway station, opened in 1844 and 1848 respectively. The 1815 battle ended the war, and forced Napoleon Bonaparte, the Emperor of France, into exile.

In February 1801, George was struck by an illness which largely repeated that of 1788, although the symptoms were not as severe on the second occasion. The king was unwell until June 1801, at which point he began a successful convalescence at Weymouth. Unfortunately the illness returned in 1804, with the result that George suffered several months of pain. He again tried rest at Weymouth, but the benefits were not as strong as in the past. George lost nearly all of the sight in his right eye, plus much of the vision from his left eye, during 1805. At the end of 1810, George experienced a further breakdown, which stemmed from grief at the death of Amelia, his youngest daughter.

The developing role of Prime Minister increased the importance, and independence, of Parliament. Having deposed Charles II in 1649, Parliament took another bold step in 1811, declaring George III unfit to rule. His son George was appointed as Prince Regent, with many of the powers of a monarch. The official king spent most of the remainder of his life in isolation, living at Windsor Castle. George III died on January 29 1820, aged 81, little more than a year after the death of his beloved Charlotte, in late 1818. The Prince Regent became George IV, reigning in his own right until he died in 1830. George was succeeded by a brother, William IV, who was king until his death in 1837.

Queen Victoria, a niece of William IV, was destined to be the British sovereign for nearly 64 years. Victoria did not, however, become the monarch of Hanover, where the operation of Salic Law excluded females from the role. Ernest Augustus, Duke of Cumberland, became king of Hanover, upon the death of his brother, William. Hanover ceased to be an independent state in 1866, being annexed by Prussia – part of a process that led to the unification of Germany in 1871. The reign of Queen Victoria saw enormous changes in British life. The continuing effects of the Industrial Revolution (a development which had coincided with the reign of George III) and the expansion of the British Empire (aided by the defeat of Napoleonic France) enabled Britain to become one of the strongest states in the world. The overall prosperity of Britain increased, but there were massive inequalities of wealth within the nation. The growth of trade unions, initially deemed illegal, improved wages, and working conditions, for millions of people.

The state started to take more of a role in the life of the ordinary person during the nineteenth century. The first British census was held in 1801, and found that the total population of England, Scotland, and Wales was 10,942,646. The census was repeated in 1811, and extended to Ireland in 1821. The full United Kingdom census has been held once every 10 years since 1821, with two exceptions. The 1921 survey excluded Ireland, due to civil war, and in 1941 the whole process was cancelled, during World War Two. The 1841 census was the first to collect detail about individuals, as opposed to merely recording total numbers. Civil registration of births, marriages, and deaths was introduced in England and Wales in 1837 – building upon the Parish Register system organised by churches since 1538. Scotland took up civil registration in 1855, and Ireland in 1864.

Extension of the limited franchise caused much debate among the narrow ruling class, with political opportunism generally outweighing principle. The Whigs extended the franchise in 1832, after a constitutional crisis, in which the Conservative members of the House of Lords used their power to defy the will of the Commons. The Conservative Party was a new name for the Tories, first used in 1830. William IV persuaded the leading Conservative peers to allow the Reform Bill to pass, to end the crisis, and gave the government a pledge to create as many peers as necessary in the event of continued obstruction. The Reform Act set the franchise, based on the annual rental value of buildings, at £10 in the boroughs, and £50 in the counties. Although their dominance had been ended, the aristocracy retained influence out of all proportion to their numbers. They had conceded some power to the middle class, but the working class remained unenfranchised.

The Reform Act dealt only with England and Wales, but equivalents for Scotland and Ireland were soon passed. Accepting the issue as settled, the Conservatives did not attempt to block the additional legislation. Once all three Acts had been passed, a General Election was held in December 1832. Newly enfranchised men rewarded the government with a majority of 288, as the combined forces of the Whigs and their allies, the Radicals, won 473 seats. The Conservatives suffered one of their worst ever electoral defeats, winning only 185 seats in a House of Commons of 658 members. The People's Charter, drawn up in 1838, advocated that the vote be given to working class men. The Chartists presented petitions to Parliament in 1839, 1842, and 1848, with millions of signatures, but legislators refused to meet the demand for fairness.

A split in the Conservative Party, from 1846, was prompted by rebellion against their Prime Minister, Robert Peel, elected in 1841, instigating repeal of the Corn Laws, which protected the income of landowners. Peel believed that famine in Ireland, stemming from failure of the potato crop, required the removal of duties on imported grain. Peel had already come to favour free trade on general grounds, but was unable to reveal this, due to the views of his party. The Irish famine lasted from 1845 until 1852. The savage policies of both Conservative and Whig governments caused the death toll in Ireland to rise to around one million people, while a similar number felt forced to emigrate. British Protestant landowners, concentrating on their own profits, were cruelly exporting food from Ireland to Britain, while the Catholic working class starved. Nowadays the actions of the British state would be condemned as genocide, and ethnic cleansing.

The widespread potato blight affected several other nations. Working class poverty – exacerbated by the shortage of potatoes – combined with desire for democracy, as opposed to autocratic monarchy, contributed to a series of attempted revolutions, in continental Europe, during 1848. At the start of that year, *The Communist Manifesto*, a pamphlet written by Karl Marx and Friedrich Engels, two philosophers from Germany, was published in London. As the revolutionary movement was suppressed, Marx and Engels went into exile, settling in England in 1849, and remaining there for the rest of their lives. Marx increasingly focussed on writing about economics, and produced a masterpiece in *Capital*, a history of the development, and laws of motion, of capitalism. This was published in three volumes, between 1867 and 1894. The second and third instalments appeared after Marx died in 1883, being edited by Engels. Much of Marx's work related to the role of Britain as the leading capitalist economy, based upon research at the British Museum in London. This included an explanation of the National Debt.

The national debt, i.e. the alienation by sale of the state – whether despotic, constitutional or republican – marked the capitalistic era with its stamp. The only part of the so-called national wealth that actually enters into the collective possession of a modern nation is their national debt. Hence, quite consistently with this, the modern doctrine that a nation becomes the richer the more deeply it is in debt. Public credit becomes the credo of capital. And with the rise of national debt-making, lack of faith in the national debt takes the place of the sin against the Holy Ghost, for which there is no forgiveness.

The National Debt has been a heavy burden upon the people of Britain for more than three centuries. As the level of debt has generally increased, capitalist speculation in one generation has been left to be funded, with mounting repayments, by future generations. In the twentieth century, financing of two world wars led to massive escalation of the National Debt. Another historic increase followed a global financial crisis, early in the twenty first century. The Conservative and Liberal Democrat coalition government inherited a national debt of £960 billion, in May 2010, and proceeded to make the situation worse. From 2015, a solely Conservative government's continued mismanagement of the economy led to the National Debt reaching £1,786 billion at the end of 2017 – an 86 per cent rise in seven and a half years. The position continued to worsen, and the total reached £2,004 billion in July 2020, during the early part of the Covid pandemic. In May 2023, the debt was £2,567 billion, exceeding the nation's annual gross domestic product for the first time since 1961. Annual interest payments on the National Debt were a massive £111 billion in the 2022-2023 financial year – this was 9.6 per cent of government spending.

Following in the footsteps of Marx, other historians have developed his analysis. Eric Hobsbawm's *Industry and Empire: From 1750 to the Present Day*, focussed on Britain, appeared in 1968, with a revised edition in 1999. The first edition of the book sold over a quarter of a million copies, an amazing total for a Marxist economic history. Hobsbawm coined the phrase "long nineteenth century" to describe the period from the French Revolution, in 1789, to the outbreak of World War One, in 1914. He argued that nineteenth century Europe was best understood within the context of major events that immediately preceded and followed it. Hobsbawm published a celebrated trilogy analysing the subject, *The Age of Revolution: Europe 1789–1848* (1962), *The Age of Capital: 1848–1875* (1975), and *The Age of Empire: 1875–1914* (1987).

Between 1847 and 1868, the Whigs and Liberals (with the latter name replacing the former from around 1859), defeated the Conservatives in six successive General Elections. Lord Derby was Prime Minister of three minority Conservative governments, in 1852, 1858-1859, and 1866-1868. Although his party were generally opposed to the idea, they saw that a successful Reform Bill could increase their public support. A Bill introduced in 1859 was not carried through Parliament. A subsequent Reform Bill was presented by a Conservative government, in 1867. The borough franchise was based on household suffrage, qualified by a number of safeguards, and the county franchise was set at a £15 rating level. The passage of the 1867 Bill saw Benjamin Disraeli, Chancellor of the Exchequer, directing operations, in brilliant style. The Bill received its Second Reading without a division. Thereafter the Conservatives' minority position in the House of Commons meant that the government had to accept a succession of Liberal amendments, which reduced the safeguards in the boroughs, and set the county franchise at £12. The government accepted the amendments so as to retain the initiative, and the Bill received its Third Reading in the Commons during July. Derby proceeded to take the scheme through the Lords without difficulty. At the Third Reading, Derby admitted, on August 6, that the measure was "a leap in the dark". In private Derby responded to a friend, who argued that the Bill was dangerous, with the question "Don't you see how we have dished the Whigs?". The Conservatives had indeed outmanoeuvred their opponents.

The Act was a major advance, but left Britain with a far from democratic franchise. The poorer urban working class, the non-urban working class, and all women, remained excluded. Successive governments refused to even consider allowing women to participate in General Elections. Extensions to the male franchise increased the strength of the House of Commons, in comparison with the House of Lords, and there was some reduction in the power of the monarchy. The Conservatives had been forced into carrying the Act by the necessity of the political situation, and were unable to protect ruling class dominance of the electorate. In the course of increasing their public support, the Conservatives attacked the social order they existed to defend.

The fortunes of the Conservatives improved during the leadership of Benjamin Disraeli (Prime Minister in 1868 and then 1874-1880), followed by Lord Salisbury (three spells as premier between 1885 and 1902). In 1875, Disraeli organised the government's purchase of Khedive Ismail's shares in the Suez Canal Company, giving Britain control of a major trading route, which led to India. In 1876 Disraeli carried the Royal Titles Act, which secured the title Empress of India for Queen Victoria. Disraeli found himself confronted with the Eastern Question. The three powers of the Dreikaiserbund – Austria, Germany, and Russia – sought to press reforms on Turkey. Disraeli felt that Britain had a legitimate interest in the relevant region. Months of negotiations, and sporadic fighting, were the result, with Britain taking the side of Turkey against Russia. A full settlement was agreed at the Congress of Berlin, during June and July 1878. Disraeli proved to be the outstanding figure at the Congress, and returned home in triumph, announcing he had secured "peace with honour". Disraeli and Salisbury glorified the monarchy and British Empire. Britain had a strength, and role in the world, far exceeding expectations for a geographically small nation, with only a tiny fraction of the global population. British influence was often negative, with violent conquest of innocent peoples, and their enslavement or economic exploitation. Supporters of the Empire argue that Britain exported ideas of justice, liberty, and constitutional government – founded in the Mother of Parliaments, sitting at Westminster – but there was little sign of democracy in this process.

The Liberals, led by William Gladstone (Prime Minister four times between 1868 and 1894), sought political and social reform. The bitter personal rivalry between Disraeli and Gladstone has become one of the most famous in British history. There is an unusual reflection in a satirical drawing by John Tenniel, imagining the two men as the Lion and the Unicorn, in battle with each other, among the illustrations to Lewis Carroll's *Through the Looking Glass, And What Alice Found There* (1871) – the sequel to *Alice's Adventures in Wonderland*. During 1884, a Liberal government overcame Conservative resistance in the Lords, and carried the Third Reform Act. This equalised the franchise between borough and county constituencies, by conferring the eligibility criteria set for the former in 1867 to the latter. Gladstone wished to introduce Home Rule for Ireland, but the first attempt to pass legislation provoked a split among the Liberals in 1886, with the Liberal Unionists becoming allies of the Conservatives.

The Democratic Federation, formed in 1881, and renamed the Social Democratic Federation (SDF) during 1884, was the first British political party to campaign for Socialism. Membership in the early years included Eleanor Marx, a daughter of Karl Marx, and William Morris, an artist and author. Morris would publish two celebrated novels, *A Dream of John Ball* (1888), dramatising the Peasants' Revolt, and *News From Nowhere* (1890), in which a future Britain became a Socialist Utopia. During 1892 Keir Hardie was elected as Britain's first independent Socialist MP. Hardie played a role in the formation of the Independent Labour Party (ILP) in 1893, along with Edward Aveling, the partner of Eleanor Marx. In 1900, the SDF and ILP, along with other left wing groups and trade unions, founded the Labour Representation Committee, with the specific aim of setting up a group to represent working people in Parliament. This was renamed the Labour Party in 1906, with Hardie as its first leader, and would replace the Liberals as the main opponent of the Conservatives during the twentieth century.

9 The Twentieth Century

Good relations between Britain and Germany, during the Hanoverian era, rapidly disintegrated in the early twentieth century. Queen Victoria was a dynastic matriarch with pan-European influence but, after her death in 1901, familial connections between monarchs became less important than the power struggle between rival empires. Victoria was succeeded by her son Edward VII, who was in turn followed by his son, George V, in 1910. Lord Salisbury, the last Prime Minister to lead a government from the House of Lords, retired in 1902. He was replaced as premier and leader of the Unionists – the name adopted by the alliance of Conservatives and Liberal Unionists, defending the enforced union of Britain and Ireland – by Arthur Balfour, his nephew. A Liberal government took office in 1905, and achieved a landslide General Election victory the following year. The Liberal programme of reform included the establishment of unemployment benefit and old age pensions, reduced power for the House of Lords, plus Home Rule for Ireland. This was bitterly resisted by the Unionists in Parliament, and in 1914 Protestant terrorists, organised by the Unionists, took Ireland to the brink of a civil war, which was only averted (or delayed) when international events took precedence.

World War One began, in August 1914, with the general mood in Britain being optimism for a quick victory. As war became protracted, Pope Benedict XV called for a Christmas truce. The idea was favoured by Germany, but opposed by Britain and its allies. Christmas Day 1914 saw an unofficial truce, on the Western Front. Men who had been fighting amidst the carnage of war briefly shared a unique Christmas celebration. There was widespread fraternisation between members of the opposing armies, and a group of German soldiers beat a British team, in one of the most poignant football matches ever played. The truce, observed at many locations, was unofficially arranged by British and German officers at a local level, in defiance of the military and political leaderships of the two countries. Attempting to raise the morale of their troops, the German authorities had sent food hampers and decorations to the trenches. With Christmas Eve being central to the holiday season in their country, the German soldiers decorated their trenches after dark that day, and sang Christmas carols. In many cases this was the action which broke the ice, and led to the truce. During Christmas Day, British and German soldiers exchanged gifts and stories about their lives. Despite great efforts, independent research by a series of historians has only managed to find a single detailed account of a match between representatives of the two armies. The match took place during Christmas Day, on a piece of waste ground between Frelinghien and

Houplines, two villages in France. The location was a just a few miles south of the Belgian town of Ypres, which gave its name to a fierce battle recently fought in this area. Johannes Niemann, a German soldier from the 133rd Royal Saxon Regiment, who participated in the game against soldiers from the Scottish Seaforth Highlanders, recalled the event in 1969, stating "the game finished with a score of three goals to two in favour of Fritz against Tommy".

The British and German troops who played football together were soon locked again in military combat. The spontaneous game on Christmas Day stands as a testament to the strength of human spirit, and the value of sportsmanship, in contrast to the brutality of war. Fifteen years later, the professional football teams of Scotland and Germany met for the first time, drawing 1-1 in Berlin, during 1929. The main British football rivalry with the Germans, however, has been the series of matches between England and Germany / West Germany. The most famous of these is the 1966 World Cup Final, in which England beat West Germany 4-2, at Wembley. During 2014 the Football Association ran a Football Remembers campaign to mark the centenary of the 1914 ceasefire. This included "The Game of Truce", a match between the British and German army teams, staged on December 17, at the ground of non-league Aldershot Town. Aldershot is the hometown of the British army, whose team achieved a 1-0 win in a spirited contest with the Germans. There was also a video produced by the Union of European Football Associations (UEFA) about the 1914 truce.

Britain played a leading role in the alliance that ultimately defeated Germany in World War One, which stretched until 1918, with four years of bloodshed. Following decades of the ruling class opposing votes for women, the efforts of the Suffragettes, and women who made a major contribution to the war effort, were rewarded, as a Unionist, Liberal, and Labour wartime coalition government carried a Representation of the People Act in 1918. This introduced full manhood suffrage, and gave the vote to women over the age of 30 who owned property. For over six hundred years prior to this, elections to Parliament had taken place without women having the vote. The age level for women receiving the vote was reduced to 21 in 1928, by the Conservatives, to match that for men. The current enfranchisement, at the age of 18, arrived as recently as 1969, with legislation from a Labour government. The vote was extended to 16 and 17 year olds in Scotland for the independence referendum of 2014, and the following year the voting age for the Scottish Parliament plus local councils was also reduced to 16. In 2021, the voting age for the Welsh Parliament was lowered to 16, but England and Northern Ireland have not embraced this reform.

A General Election, held on December 14 1918, returned a Unionist and Liberal coalition government to power. The largest opposition party was Sinn Fein, committed to independence for Ireland, but its 73 MPs refused to take their seats in a Parliament they did not recognise as legitimate. These included Constance Markievicz, the first woman elected to the House of Commons, despite her being held in a British prison – as a result of opposition to the conscription of Irish people to fight in the war. Upon her release, Markievicz became a member of the revolutionary government in Ireland. Civil war led to partition in 1922, with Northern Ireland remaining in the United Kingdom, while the majority of the territory, named the Irish Free State, would become the Republic of Ireland. In 1919, Nancy Astor, a Unionist, became the first woman MP to take her seat in the Commons. Nancy Astor was elected at Plymouth Drake, in succession to her husband Waldorf Astor, on his moving to the House of Lords. Waldorf became Viscount Astor in succession to his father, William Waldorf Astor, a businessman from the USA, who had been admitted into the British peerage.

During the troubled period between two world wars, from 1918 to 1939, the Conservative Party held power, either alone or as the dominant partner in a coalition, for 18 years. The exception was the two short minority Labour governments, led by Ramsey MacDonald. The first of these was defeated at a General Election, in 1924, with the Conservative attack being helped by the appearance of the Zinoviev letter. This forgery was alleged to have been written by the President of the Communist International, Zinoviev, to the British Communist Party, advising them on tactics. The next Labour administration struggled in the face of the worldwide capitalist crisis (the "Great Depression"), which spread from the USA after 1929. As the state of public finances deteriorated, the Cabinet, under pressure from the financial sector (the "Bankers' Ramp"), were split on what action to take. On August 24 1931 MacDonald resigned as Prime Minister, disbanding the Labour government, and was immediately reappointed, by George V, as the head of a coalition. The Conservatives and Liberals agreed to participate in this National Government, but MacDonald was only able to carry a minority of his colleagues, who founded the National Labour Party.

The early weeks of the National Government's term of office saw drastic measures, to address the immediate financial crisis. The new administration decided to fight a General Election on a coalition basis, with polling day being October 27. The government won 554 seats – including 473 Conservatives – and a majority of 491. The opposition was led by the official Labour Party, reduced to only 52 MPs, despite getting 29 per cent of the popular vote. Ramsey MacDonald remained the premier, displaying diminishing abilities, and Stanley Baldwin, the Conservative leader, held effective control of the government. Neville Chamberlain, another Conservative, became Chancellor of the Exchequer. The government failed in economic terms, and unemployment remained at above one million people throughout its period in office.

In 1933, Adolf Hitler, and the Nazi Party, seized power in Germany. The Conservatives were slow to realise the threat, as many of them, notably Winston Churchill, a former Chancellor of the Exchequer, admired Hitler's nationalist approach. They saw Fascism, an authoritarian version of Conservatism, as preferable to democracy and Socialism. The Conservatives had supported Benito Mussolini's Fascist dictatorship in Italy, ever since it took power in 1922. Ramsey MacDonald stepped down as Prime Minister, and was replaced by Baldwin, on June 7 1935. Meanwhile the government concluded an Anglo-German Naval Agreement, which provided for the limitation of the German force in relation to the British navy. This conflicted with the government's support for the League of Nations, and collective security. An Election was held on November 14, and the National Government retained power, with 429 MPs – of whom 388 were Conservatives – and a majority of 243 seats. The Labour Party, taking 38 per cent of the vote, increased its strength to 154 seats. With Germany becoming increasingly aggressive, the National Government planned rearmament, but was not decisive in its approach.

George V died in January 1936, being succeeded by Edward VIII. Baldwin was suffering poor health, but decided to remain as Prime Minister to help the new king, putting the Conservative Party's reverence for the monarchy before the interests of the British people. Baldwin saw a worsening international situation, but did not take effective action. In March, Germany reoccupied the Rhineland, and the National Government declined to confront Hitler over this. During May, Italy completed the conquest of Abyssinia, and the National Government decided against the continuation of sanctions, agreed by the League of Nations, against Italy. In July, the Spanish Civil War broke out, as General Franco led an army revolt, against a freely elected Socialist and radical government. MI6 supported Franco in launching the rebellion, acting on behalf of the British ruling class, who were concerned that democratic government in Spain was not good for capitalism. The Conservatives signed an international non-intervention agreement in respect of Spain, but failed to secure its operation. This allowed Italy and Germany to support Franco's attempts to impose Fascism.

Edward VIII wished to marry Wallis Simpson, an American divorcee, but was barred by law from doing so while he was king. Edward had friendly links with the Nazi Party, and the government knew that Mrs Simpson was having an affair with Joachim von Ribbentrop, the German Ambassador to Britain. The king and his mistress were also leaking British government secrets to Hitler's regime. Baldwin delegated much of the work required to lead the government to Neville Chamberlain, who displayed terrible complacency by letting his London house to von Ribbentrop. Edward chose to abdicate, to be free to marry, and maintained links with the Nazis for several years. Baldwin remained in office, to again see a new monarch, George VI, settle into the role. Baldwin finally departed in May 1937, and his retirement was accompanied by that of Ramsey MacDonald. Neville Chamberlain became Prime Minister, and rearmament gained momentum, but his major preoccupation was the appeasement of Germany and Italy. Anthony Eden, the Foreign Secretary, an equivocal supporter of appeasement, resigned in February 1938, being replaced by Lord Halifax, who was clearly pro-German. In March, Germany annexed Austria.

The majority of Conservatives supported appeasement in the hope it would prevent war, but they also had sympathy for Fascism. There were prominent roles for members of the party in the Anglo-German Fellowship, the Friends of Italy, and the Friends of National Spain. Support for Fascism by the British governing party demoralised the democratic forces in Italy, Germany, and Spain. Chamberlain thought Hitler was justified in wishing to take part of Czechoslovakia, and announced that Britain should not go to war over "a quarrel in a far away country between people of whom we know nothing". Hitler agreed to host a conference on the issue, at Munich, bringing together the governments of Germany, Italy, Britain, and France, but excluding the Czechs. On September 30, the conference agreed Germany could annex the German-populated areas of Czechoslovakia, while the integrity of the remainder would be guaranteed by the powers. Chamberlain returned to Britain waving a piece of paper, on which was written a statement – drawn up after the main agreement – in which he and Hitler expressed the wishes of their countries to settle disputes by negotiation, and avoid war. Chamberlain announced that he had secured "peace with honour" – a phrase Benjamin Disraeli had used after the Congress of Berlin in 1878 – and "peace for our time". This belief proved tragically wrong, and the Conservatives were content to see the people of Austria and Czechoslovakia condemned to Nazi tyranny.

At the end of February 1939, the National Government prematurely recognised Franco as the ruler of Spain. The Spanish Civil War was not to be finally decided in Franco's favour until a few weeks later. In March, Germany overran Czechoslovakia. It looked likely that Germany would move against Poland. Chamberlain finally made a stand, giving the Polish government a guarantee of national independence. Hitler responded by renouncing the Anglo-German Naval Agreement. An unenthusiastic attempt, by the National Government, to secure an alliance with the Soviet Union followed. The opposition of the Conservatives to the Soviet Union led to the government's failure to secure an alliance that it saw as desirable. In August, Germany secured a non-aggression pact with the Soviet Union. At the beginning of the following month, Germany invaded Poland. After some hesitation, Chamberlain issued an ultimatum to Germany, on September 3, ordering them to withdraw from Poland or face war. The Germans did not respond so Chamberlain declared war that same day. He secured the resignation of the National Government, which had completed its calamitous course, and ceased to exist. Britain faced a war for which it was not prepared.

Britain's role in a coalition of Allies, which defeated Fascism in World War Two, remains a justifiable source of national pride. Nazi Germany threatened to enslave Britain, and much of the world, with a systematic programme of racism and genocide. The Nazis – working with the rulers of the other Axis powers, Italy and Japan – posed an unprecedented threat to progress and human civilisation. Amidst celebration of the eventual British victory, there has too often been a tendency to forget the incompetence, and often deliberate treachery, of a ruling class that developed the policy of appeasement.

Chamberlain formed a new government in September 1939, and Churchill was appointed First Lord of the Admiralty. A series of blunders culminated in the disaster of the Norway campaign, at the beginning of May 1940. Churchill was primarily responsible for this setback. In a Commons debate on the failure in Norway, Labour forced a vote. The government's majority was reduced to 81, as opposed to the usual figure of over 200, with 33 Conservative MPs voting against their government, while 60 abstained. This represented the equivalent of a defeat for Chamberlain, who resigned as premier, but remained leader of the Conservative Party. Churchill became Prime Minister, securing the position at the expense of Lord Halifax, despite his role in the Norway expedition. Most Conservatives would have preferred Halifax, who remained sympathetic to the Nazis, and had recently supported attempts to negotiate a peace with Hitler. Churchill formed a coalition, which included members of the Labour and Liberal parties as well as the Conservatives. The discredited Chamberlain remained in the Cabinet, as Lord President. Victory seemed far away as the disaster in Norway was followed by catastrophe in France, at the end of May, when allied troops had to be evacuated from Dunkirk. The Summer and early Autumn saw the British air victory against the Germans, in the Battle of Britain. Ill health forced Chamberlain to leave the government, at the end of September. Churchill made it clear that he wished to be the leader of the Conservatives, and his position as Prime Minister gained him the post. Chamberlain resigned the leadership, and a meeting to elect Churchill was held on October 9. Chamberlain died a few weeks later.

The Germans launched the Blitz in the Autumn of 1940, and this was to last through the Winter. On June 22 1941, Germany invaded the Soviet Union, and this reduced the effectiveness of the former. On December 7, Japan entered the war, attacking the United States fleet at Pearl Harbour. With Germany and Japan now becoming allied, the United States entered the war alongside Britain. The danger of defeat for Britain in the war reduced, but victory remained a long way off. Domestic politics was largely put on hold, but there was some preparation for the future. This process began with the investigation into social security by Sir William Beveridge. The Beveridge Report, published in December 1942, envisaged a comprehensive scheme of social security. The plan was originally due to come into effect in July 1944. The Conservative Party was not, however, enthusiastic about the scheme so the government delayed implementation.

In June 1942, Britain formed an alliance with the Soviet Union, which in turn led to an unlikely friendship between the respective leaders, Churchill and Stalin. Churchill appeared to have a penchant for ruthless dictators. Churchill was able to lead Britain to victory in the war, but this was achieved at a terrible cost in human life. The eventual combined death toll for British service personnel and civilians in World War Two was around 500,000 people. Churchill was racist, with a particular hatred for the people of India. His decision to divert food away from the population of Bengal, and towards the British army fighting in the region, turned the Bengal Famine into an act of genocide, in which over two million Indian people died of starvation during 1943.

The D-Day Allied landings in northern France occurred on June 6 1944, and thereafter the war went favourably for Britain. Germany surrendered on May 8 1945, ending the war in Europe. Churchill wished the Coalition to continue until Japan was defeated, an event that was not expected to occur until the following year. This was subsequently hastened by the USA dropping atomic bombs on Hiroshima and Nagasaki, in August 1945, deliberately killing a vast number of civilians, whereupon Japan surrendered. The Labour members of the Cabinet wanted an Election on party lines to take place in the Autumn, whereupon Churchill insisted it be held as soon as possible. He resigned on behalf of the government on May 23, and was reappointed by the king, to head a caretaker Conservative administration. Polling was set for

July 5 but, with many electors abroad with the services, the count was delayed, and the results not announced until July 26. Churchill concentrated on attacking the imaginary intentions of the Labour Party, claiming it would not be able to implement its programme without "some form of Gestapo", a sickening reference to the Nazi secret police, which had terrorised opponents in Germany. Labour won 393 seats, and a majority of 146, as people voted for new hope. The discredited Conservative Party took only 198 seats in the 1945 Election – their smallest total between defeats by the Liberals in 1906, and Labour in 1997.

The Labour Party formed its first majority government in 1945, with Clement Attlee as Prime Minister. Labour carried a major programme of reform, moving Britain towards economic democracy, with public ownership of the Bank of England, coal mines, railways, electricity, gas, and steel, combined with delivery of a welfare state. In 1946, the Conservatives repeatedly voted against the legislation to set up the National Health Service, stirring up groundless fears about the scheme. With Aneurin Bevan, the Labour Minister of Health who guided the plan, standing firm, the NHS opened on July 5 1948. On the previous day, Bevan made a speech, at Manchester, asserting the historic value of the government's programme. He said:

The eyes of the world are turning to Great Britain. We now have the moral leadership of the world, and before many years are over we shall have people coming here as to a modern Mecca, learning from us in the twentieth century as they learned from us in the seventeenth century.

Bevan was an enthusiastic Marxist, who saw Parliamentary rebellion against the monarchy, in the 1640s, as an important step in the road towards democracy in Britain. Bevan's role also included responsibility for housing, and he organised the building of a million council houses, to a higher standard than was previously in place. Council houses remained a central part of affordable accommodation in Britain, until there was a reversal of policy in the 1980s. Other elements of the British post-war dream also faded, but political advances begun in 1945 improved the quality of life for the majority of a population that was rapidly increasing, with improved life expectancy. Across the span of a century, the total of 41,458,721 people, recorded in the 1901 United Kingdom census (including the whole of Ireland), became the 58,789,194 people declared in the 2001 equivalent (featuring Northern Ireland).

The Labour government was re-elected in 1950, but with a majority of only five seats. This was the first General Election to be held on a one person one vote basis. Labour had abolished the unfair system of plural votes – beloved of wealthy Conservatives – in the Representation of the People Act 1948. Another Election followed in 1951, and this time the Conservatives gained a majority of 17 seats, although Labour won the popular vote, with a clear endorsement of the radical programme implemented during six years in office. Labour's poll of 13,948,385 was a higher vote than any party achieved at a British General Election prior to that date – this total would not be exceeded by any party until 1992.

Winston Churchill returned to the post of Prime Minister in 1951, and held the role until 1955, despite declining health, largely due to his wish to work with the new monarch. The reign of Elizabeth II, who took the throne in 1952, was to become the longest ever by a British sovereign, reaching 70 years a few months before her death in 2022. The political influence of the monarchy reduced, amidst strengthened republican feeling. However, appointment of a premier remained the sole preserve of the monarch. The antiquated, and unwritten, British constitution – in which trust of those in power is supposed to make up for lack of legal democratic guarantees – led to controversy over the process for appointment of a Prime Minister, in the event of a hung Parliament. This scenario occurred three times during the reign of Elizabeth, in 1974, 2010, and 2017.

Churchill was followed as premier by Anthony Eden, and the latter was responsible for the Suez debacle in 1956. This was an unsuccessful attempt to regain control of the Suez Canal, which had been British-owned, but was nationalised by Egypt. Military forces from Britain and France invaded Egypt, in collusion with Israel. Eden misled Parliament, claiming "there was no foreknowledge that Israel would attack Egypt – there was not", as he had reached a secret invasion agreement with the government of Israel. The Conservatives held power until 1964, a period that became known as "thirteen years of Tory misrule". The third Prime Minister in this spell, Harold Macmillan, took office in 1957, replacing Eden. With many colonies achieving independence from the British Empire, nationalists lamented a decline of Britain's economic and military strength, relative to other powerful states. Macmillan's hope of Britain joining the European Economic Community was blocked by France, at the start of 1963. As the Empire gave way to the Commonwealth, many people from British territories in the Caribbean, Africa, and Asia came here to work. These people settled in Britain, and their communities became integrated. Unfortunately the "hostile environment", directed by Conservative governments from 2010 onwards, towards illegal immigrants spilled over into racist mistreatment of legal migrants. The revelations of the Windrush Scandal, in 2018, showed that many people who had arrived from the Caribbean islands, decades earlier, were having their British citizenship removed. They were descended from some of the millions of people forcibly transported from Africa to the Caribbean, as slave labour, by inhuman British entrepreneurs – backed by the state – mostly during the seventeenth and eighteenth centuries.

Macmillan resigned in the Autumn of 1963, largely due to the events of the Profumo Scandal, which had come to a head in the Summer. John Profumo, the Minister for War, had an affair with Christine Keeler, at a time when she in turn was having an affair with Eugene Ivanov, a spy masquerading as a naval attache at the Soviet Union's embassy. Profumo denied an affair with Keeler, in a statement to the Commons, but subsequently admitted that he had lied, and resigned as an MP. The government faced allegations about a possible breach of security. Macmillan mishandled the question, lightly accepting Profumo's original denial. The Profumo Scandal exerted fascination for decades, and was brilliantly dramatised in the film *Scandal*, released in 1989. Macmillan was replaced as premier by Lord Home, an out of touch aristocrat, and the Conservatives lost to Labour in the 1964 General Election.

Harold Wilson was Prime Minister of a Labour government from 1964 to 1970, and also held that post from 1974 to 1976, at which point he was replaced by James Callaghan. These administrations combined modernisation of the economy with social reform, including measures to make racial and sexual discrimination illegal. Britain joined the EEC at the start of 1973, on the initiative of a Conservative government, led by Edward Heath. A substantial number of Conservatives refused to back entry into the EEC, and Heath only managed to pass the European Communities Act 1972 with the help of some Labour MPs, who rebelled against their party's position. Heath saw entry into the EEC as a major benefit for Britain, and was prepared to accept the loss of Britain's independence. The laws of Britain ceased to be the sole preserve of its Parliament, as they became subject to those of the EEC. Following the imposition of three day working weeks, aimed at reducing consumption of electricity, and amidst a strike by coal miners, Heath called an Election, set for February 28 1974. With this resulting in a hung Parliament, Heath stayed in office, attempting to form a coalition, although Labour had won more seats than the Conservatives. Heath's negotiations with the Liberals broke down, over their insistence on proportional representation. Heath resigned on March 4, and Harold Wilson formed a minority Labour government. A second Election was held on October 10, and Labour won a majority of 3.

The Labour government renegotiated the terms of British EEC membership, and submitted the deal to the people in a referendum, during 1975. The outcome was a vote for the United Kingdom remaining in the EEC, with improved terms, by a margin of 67 per cent to 33 per cent. Tony Benn, a radical member of the Labour government, persuaded his Cabinet colleagues that the decision on membership should be delegated to a direct vote by the people. Benn, one of the most articulate advocates of withdrawal from the EEC, continued to be influential in this cause through until his death, in 2014.

In 1979 the Conservative Party returned to power, with Margaret Thatcher as Prime Minister. Thatcher proclaimed herself a "conviction politician", opposed to consensus. Her major preoccupation was an attempt to revive the free market, through monetarism – developed by Milton Friedman, an economist from the USA. Monetarism was a theory that had only been properly tested by one of the world's most barbaric regimes, the Fascist military dictatorship in Chile, and the result had been a spectacular failure. Thatcher's government soon proved a calamity for Britain, with a strategy of reduced public expenditure, reduced taxation – especially for the wealthy – an attack on the trade unions, and the sale of public assets. When Thatcher took power, more than a million people were unemployed. The number of unemployed people increased to two million in August 1980, and three million in January 1982. The sale of council houses was introduced in 1980, along with financial restrictions, that effectively prevented local authorities from using the proceeds to fund the building of new homes. The policy fuelled a growth in prices and rents, plus homelessness, the sad legacy of which continues to afflict potential owners and tenants today.

The Thatcher government became increasingly unpopular, until its fortunes were revived by victory in the Falklands War. The Argentinian invasion of the Falkland Islands, in 1982, represented a crisis. Britain was responsible for defence of the Falklands, as a Crown Colony (relic of the Empire) – a name changed to British Dependent Territory the following year, and British Overseas Territory in 2002. The military operation to recover the islands reflected well on Thatcher. Her position was also helped by a split in the Labour Party. A group of MPs on the Labour right formed the Social Democratic Party, in 1981. The SDP subsequently worked with the Liberal Party, in an Alliance, which took a huge number of votes off Labour at the next Election. The Conservatives won General Elections in 1983 and 1987, with majorities of 144 and 100 seats respectively, but fell into crisis. The Autumn of 1990 brought division among the Cabinet over Britain joining the EEC's Exchange Rate Mechanism. Michael Heseltine, a former Cabinet Minister, challenged Thatcher for the Conservative Party leadership. On the first ballot, Thatcher was close to victory, but was soon persuaded by Cabinet colleagues that she had lost the confidence of the Parliamentary party. John Major, the Chancellor of the Exchequer, emerged as the party leader, and Prime Minister.

Within a few weeks, Major took Britain into the Gulf War, committing the armed forces to support the USA in attacking Iraq, at the start of 1991, following the Iraqi invasion of Kuwait the previous year. An international coalition defeated Iraq in the war, and liberated the Kuwaiti oil fields, for the benefit of the western world. A few months later, the Soviet Union disintegrated, starting the process whereby Russia and the other members of the union became separate states. This was presented in the west as the defeat of Communism, and the end of the Cold War. Eric Hobsbawm saw the event as of such significance that it became the closing point for *The Age of Extremes: The Short Twentieth Century 1914–1991*, published in 1994, as a sequel to his "long nineteenth century" trilogy. Hobsbawm was by now revered as one of the greatest historians in the world, leading to the book being translated into thirty languages.

A General Election was held in April 1992. For much of the campaign it appeared likely Labour would win, but John Major and the Conservatives retained power. The Conservative majority was reduced to 21 seats, although the party's vote of 14,093,007 remains the highest ever for a single party in the UK. In September 1992, currency speculation forced the withdrawal of Sterling from the Exchange Rate Mechanism. Conservative economic failure caused unemployment to exceed three million people in February 1993. Major presided over an increasingly weakened government, with the Conservatives divided over the transfer of powers to the European Union, as the EEC was re-branded in 1993, in line with the Maastricht Treaty, signed the previous year. Major narrowly avoided defeat in the House of Commons over the legislation to implement the treaty, due to the "Maastricht Rebels" group of Conservative MPs. In his frustration, Major was overheard telling a television interviewer, when he thought the microphones were off, about the problems caused by Eurosceptic "bastards" in his Cabinet. The United Kingdom Independence Party (UKIP) was formed, to campaign for withdrawal from the EU. The government's majority was gradually eroded, due to By-Election defeats, along with withdrawal of the whip from rebellious MPs, leading to the Conservatives being placed in a minority from 1996. Major delayed calling a General Election until the end of a five year term, at which point the Conservatives were reduced to 165 seats, their smallest total since 1906. Labour won a landslide victory even bigger than that of 1945, with the majority in 1997 being 179 seats, and Tony Blair became Prime Minister.

10 A New Millennium

Britain entered a new millennium in 2000, at a time of changes in the nation's political arrangements which appeared likely to be of lasting significance. The current era has seen much debate on the state of the United Kingdom, with questions about its future. Positive devolution of power from the Westminster Parliament – situated in England – to legislative bodies in Scotland, Wales, and Northern Ireland, has been accompanied by negative speculation. Unionists speak of fears that the United Kingdom may lose long-established traditions. They fail to recognise that the United Kingdom of Great Britain and Ireland was formed relatively recently, in 1801. The present name, the United Kingdom of Great Britain and Northern Ireland, stems from 1927, five years after the majority of Ireland became independent. There is also much constitutional argument about the implications of the European referendum of 2016. The majority of the vote across the United Kingdom was in favour of leaving the European Union, but within this total most of the votes cast in both Scotland and Northern Ireland favoured remaining in the EU. Supporters of the United Kingdom refer to a "family of nations", but the dominance of England has led to increasing nationalist feeling in Scotland, similar stirrings in Wales, and growing discussion about reunification of Ireland.

The Scottish Parliament and National Assembly for Wales (the native name being Cynulliad Cenedlaethol Cymru) were both set up in 1999. This initiative, proposed by the Labour government elected in 1997, was approved in separate referendums by the people of Scotland and Wales, and Acts of the United Kingdom Parliament. The devolved bodies successfully implemented a measure of self-government, which continues to develop. In 2020, the legislature in Wales was renamed the Welsh Parliament / Senedd Cymru. There have been improvements to the political situation in Northern Ireland, and the virtual ending of terrorist violence there. The Belfast Agreement, generally known as the Good Friday agreement, was reached between the governments of Britain and the Republic of Ireland, in April 1998. This was endorsed in parallel referendums, by the people of both Northern Ireland and the Republic of Ireland. The Northern Ireland Assembly, created in 1999, began to take responsibility for devolved government, bringing together Catholics and Protestants. Disputes among the participants led to a lengthy suspension of the assembly, from October 2002 through to May 2007. The resumption of devolved government saw the establishment of a power-sharing administration, comprising the Democratic Unionist Party and Sinn Fein – a situation unthinkable a few years earlier.

The House of Lords Act 1999, following a Labour manifesto pledge to reform the unelected chamber of Parliament, removed most of the hereditary members. A group of 92 hereditary peers – selected by their heading a ballot amongst that group – were allowed to remain in their lordships' house, as part of a compromise deal. Abolition, or further reform, of the Lords was discussed in Parliament several times over the next few years, with continuing government pledges to advance the process, without any changes being agreed. Retention of archaic tradition means that Britain, in the twenty first century, has one of the few remaining monarchies in the world, and still accords a place in its law-making to the unelected House of Lords.

Robin Cook, the Labour Foreign Secretary in 1997, announced "our foreign policy must have an ethical dimension", including support for democracy and human rights. After an impressive start, policy became increasingly tied to that of George W Bush, the President of the USA, and son of George H W Bush, the leader who had launched the first Gulf War in 1991. During Tony Blair's premiership, Britain was involved in a series of military conflicts, in Yugoslavia, Afghanistan, and Iraq. The period since the end of World War Two had seen several decades of relative peace throughout Europe. The most significant exception was the Yugoslav Civil War, fought between 1991 and 2001, with nationalist conflict causing division of the country into successor states. Blair agreed to British involvement in NATO bombing of Yugoslavia, during 1999, in support of the people of Kosovo, but the legality of this was doubtful.

Labour won a second landslide victory in the June 2001 General Election, with a majority of 167 seats – just 12 seats less than four years earlier. After offering new direction, following 18 years of Conservative rule, Labour lost momentum. Blair's reputation was damaged by a perception that the government had exchanged honesty for the tales of "spin doctors". The handling of the Iraq war, in the Spring of 2003, and its aftermath, particularly undermined Blair's standing. The case for participation in the war against Iraq hinged on the claim that the dictator, Saddam Hussein, was readily able to deploy weapons of mass destruction. A BBC report, by Andrew Gilligan, suggested the government had exaggerated the extent of the threat from the Iraqis. This led to a major row between the government and BBC. Gilligan received information from David Kelly, a civil servant at the Ministry of Defence, who tragically committed suicide, as his role became known. An enquiry, chaired by Lord Hutton, investigated the matter at length, with evidence being published on the enquiry's website, in keeping with the spirit of the Freedom of Information Act 2000 – introduced by the Labour government to provide much better access to information about public services. Hutton's report, issued at the start of 2004, was a whitewash, which cleared the government, and blamed the BBC. The British military role in Iraq continued until 2009, aimed at helping internal peace, in the face of sectarian violence. This led to the deaths of 179 British servicemen and women. Impassioned political and media debate, plus public protest, surrounded Britain's role, as protracted conflict caused the deaths of several hundred thousand Iraqi people.

The Labour government secured a third term in office, at the May 2005 General Election, but with a diminished majority of 66. Tony Blair stepped down as Prime Minister in 2007, and was replaced by Gordon Brown, the new Labour leader, who had been Chancellor of the Exchequer for a decade. Brown faced the onset of a financial crisis, largely caused by the speculative activities of banks, which intensified during 2008, becoming a global recession. This was the biggest failure of capitalism since the "Great Depression" that began in 1929. Brown oversaw the part-nationalisation of some British banks, and co-ordinated international efforts to tackle the crisis. The vast amounts of public money used to rescue private sector banks left the government with a large budget deficit. Blaming Labour for events beyond their control, the Conservatives gained ground. The latter were led by David Cameron, who was elected to the role in late 2005, little more than four years after he first became an MP. Public confidence in the political system was severely reduced by the scandal of MPs making excessive, often illegal, claims for expenses. After requests under the Freedom of Information Act had been blocked, due to lengthy resistance by MPs, the *Daily Telegraph* leaked information, during 2009.

The General Election of May 2010 produced a hung Parliament. The Conservatives were the largest party, ahead of Labour, with the Liberal Democrats in third place. The Conservative Party had failed to win a majority for a fourth successive Election, which represented their worst sequence of results since six successive defeats between 1847 and 1868. During five days of negotiations at Westminster, Gordon Brown resigned as leader of the Labour Party, attempting to provide a fresh start, from which the government might be able to stay in power, with Liberal Democrats joining the administration. Harriet Harman took the role of acting leader of the Labour Party, but Brown's manoeuvre did not work. David Cameron, leader of the Conservatives, arranged a political marriage with the Liberal Democrats, and the two parties formed a coalition government. Cameron became the Prime Minister, with Nick Clegg, a Lib Dem, as Deputy. Cameron, aged 43, was the youngest premier since Lord Liverpool, a Tory who took office in 1812.

The coalition carried out deep public spending cuts, with austerity reducing public services, but did not revive the economy. Unemployment increased to almost 2,700,000 by the end of 2011 – the highest figure since 1994. A messy compromise between the Conservatives, who opposed electoral reform, and the Liberal Democrats, who had long been in favour, led to a referendum on the generally unsatisfactory Alternative Vote, in May 2011. The electorate rejected AV by 68 per cent to 32 per cent, a result which damaged the cause of electoral reform. Later that year the coalition carried legislation to set a fixed term of five years for Parliament – unless there was a vote of no confidence in the government, or a majority vote of two thirds of MPs in favour of an early Election. It appeared the main motive was a wish by the coalition government to bind the two parties in the alliance, with a law forcing them to remain in power for five years.

An independence referendum was held in Scotland, on the initiative of the Scottish National Party administration. In the weeks leading up to polling in September 2014, the Conservatives were worried that the outcome would be a vote to leave the United Kingdom. With the coalition government unpopular in Scotland, they left much of the detailed Unionist campaigning to the Labour Party, with Gordon Brown taking centre-stage. The referendum rejected independence, at this point, by a margin of 55 per cent to 45 per cent. The next General Election was held in May 2015, with opinion polls pointing to another hung Parliament, but the Conservatives won a majority, for the first time since 1992. The Conservative majority of 12 stemmed from their getting only 37 per cent of the votes cast. The Conservatives won 331 seats, while Labour were reduced to 232 seats. The Scottish National Party, with 56 MPs, replaced the Liberal Democrats as the third largest party.

Cameron announced, in February 2016, that a planned referendum on membership of the European Union would be held on June 23. Through most of the campaign the mainstream media, and opinion polls, pointed to a vote to remain in the EU, the position supported by Cameron and most of his Cabinet. During the early hours of June 24, the results were declared, and it gradually became clear that the British people had voted to leave the EU, with the final margin being 52 per cent to 48 per cent. Cameron had said that, in the event of this happening, he would promptly invoke Article 50, starting the formal process of taking Britain out of the European Union. Instead of this, Cameron announced his resignation as soon as the referendum result was known. He was replaced by Theresa May as Prime Minister, and leader of the Conservatives.

May's mantra was "Brexit Means Brexit", but she would not commit to a timetable. There was a successful legal challenge to the government claim that Article 50 could be invoked by Royal Prerogative, and specific legislation had to be carried before the decision was notified to the European Union, in March 2017. A snap General Election followed on

June 8, after May won a vote in the House of Commons to over-ride the Fixed Term Parliament Act timetable. May had consistently denied suggestions that she would call an early Election, but now asked for a personal mandate for Brexit. The Labour Party, inspired by the radical Socialist leadership of Jeremy Corbyn, made gains, and the Conservatives lost their majority. May clung to power, her minority government propped up by the misnamed Democratic Unionist Party – which had links to Unionist terrorism. This alliance exacerbated the political crisis in Northern Ireland, following recent suspension of the Assembly, caused by a major dispute between the Democratic Unionist Party and Sinn Fein. This break in the functioning of the Assembly was destined to last three years, from January 2017 until January 2020. There were major concerns that a lack of clarity about the future links between Northern Ireland and the Republic of Ireland – including a possible "hard border" – could undermine the peace process.

Brexit was aimed at "taking back control" of the British economy, and law-making process. There was a strong undercurrent of xenophobia, and racism, among some elements of the project. The Conservatives were slow to guarantee the rights of citizens from other European Union nations, already settled in Britain. Theresa May finally reached a withdrawal agreement with the EU in November 2018. The government failed to comply with a resolution of the House of Commons, instructing them to issue legal advice they received on the withdrawal agreement. On December 4, a further resolution of the Commons found government ministers to be in contempt of Parliament – an unprecedented rebuke. A week later, May unilaterally postponed a Commons vote on the withdrawal agreement, following three days of debate, admitting that her government would have been defeated. A group of Conservative MPs forced a possible vote of no confidence in May as leader of the party. This was held on December 12, with May winning by 200 votes to 117, after offering to stand down prior to the next General Election, but over a third of Conservative MPs had tried to bring her down immediately.

The delayed vote on the withdrawal agreement arrived on January 15 2019, amidst high drama, as the House of Commons rejected May's Brexit deal by 432 votes to 202 – the margin of 230 being the biggest ever Parliamentary defeat for a British government. Jeremy Corbyn immediately announced that he was tabling a vote of no confidence in May's government. This motion was defeated the following day, by a margin of 325 to 306, with May only avoiding defeat due to the votes of DUP MPs. May brought back her deal on March 12, and it was defeated in the Commons by 391 votes to 242 – a massive margin of 149 votes. May reluctantly agreed a short Article 50 extension with the rest of the EU, having been directed to do so by Parliament, thereby having to renege on her frequent assurances that Brexit would take place on March 29. Instead that date saw May's third Commons defeat on the withdrawal agreement, by 344 votes to 286 – the scale of defeat now being 58 votes. During April, May was even more reluctantly forced to accept a longer delay to Brexit, offered by the EU, until the end of October 2019 (if a deal was not ratified earlier), to prevent an immediate departure without a deal. Britain participated in elections to the EU Parliament, held in late May, and Theresa May announced a protracted timetable for her departure as premier.

A Conservative Party leadership contest saw Boris Johnson emerge as the winner, a year after he resigned as Foreign Secretary – in a disagreement with Cabinet colleagues over Brexit strategy. Johnson was appointed Prime Minister by Elizabeth II on July 24, having given an untested assurance that he commanded a majority in the House of Commons. Johnson was widely distrusted, due to his serial dishonesty and incompetence, plus racist, sexist, and homophobic comments. May had failed to deliver an exit from the EU, more than three years after the referendum, but Johnson claimed departure would happen on October 31, a date just over three months away.

In August, Jacob Rees-Mogg, Leader of the House of Commons, obtained agreement from the monarch to prorogue Parliament, for five weeks, leading up to a planned Queen's Speech in mid-October. It was generally believed that Johnson and the government were seeking to prevent Parliament scrutinising Brexit plans, and legal challenges began. In early September, Parliament passed what became known as the Benn Act – introduced by Hilary Benn, a Labour MP, and son of Tony – requiring the Prime Minister to seek a further extension to Brexit if, by October 19, Parliament had not approved either a withdrawal agreement or a no deal departure. The combined Conservative and DUP MPs were now in a minority position in the Commons, and the government was defeated on several substantive votes. Johnson, acting with increasing irrationality, said "I'd rather be dead in a ditch" when asked if he would seek an extension. In late September, after Parliament had been prorogued for two weeks, the Supreme Court ruled the government's action unlawful, and the legislature resumed sitting.

On October 19, Parliament met on a Saturday (for the first time since the Falklands War, 37 years earlier), to consider an amended agreement, which the government had reached with the EU. The Commons voted to delay any approval until the necessary legislation had been passed. Johnson sent the letter to the EU required by the Benn Act, but petulantly refused to sign it, and also sent a contradictory letter, arguing against an extension. Three days later, the Commons gave a second reading to the Withdrawal Agreement Bill, but rejected a government attempt to rush it through Parliament. Johnson announced a pause in this legislative process, and was forced to agree with the EU that Brexit would be delayed for a third time, probably until the end of January 2020. With the extension in place, Johnson got the agreement of the House of Commons, at the fourth attempt, to an early General Election. With polling date set as December 12 2019, Britain entered its first Winter Election since February 1974 – and the first such contest in December since 1923.

The campaign opened with the government preventing release of a report, from the House of Commons Intelligence and Security Committee, on growing interference in British politics by Russia. This included large scale funding of the Conservative Party by Russian Oligarchs. The report finally appeared the following Summer. The Conservatives sought to make Brexit the main Election issue, and were helped by the Brexit Party, set up by Nigel Farage (previously leader of the now rapidly declining UKIP), not opposing sitting Conservative MPs. Labour proposed a programme that would end austerity, and rebuild the NHS plus other public services. They aimed to negotiate an improved deal with the EU, and put this to a second referendum, with an option to remain rather than leave. When the results were announced, the Conservatives had 365 MPs, and an 80 seat majority. Labour were reduced to 202 MPs, their lowest total since 1935, largely due to the loss of support in areas that voted to leave the EU. Despite proclamations from Farage, who lacked the courage to actually stand as a candidate, the Brexit Party failed to win any seats.

The Johnson's government EU Withdrawal Agreement Bill became law eight days before the UK left the European Union, the latter event taking place on January 31 2020. This ended the era of EEC / EU membership, which had lasted 47 years, and the UK entered a transition period, due to expire at the end of 2020. The first UK cases of the Covid-19 Coronavirus pandemic were diagnosed on the day that Brexit took place. The government, particularly Matt Hancock, the Health Secretary, took little action to alert the public to the scale of the danger. Pressure from NHS staff, opposition parties, scientists, and the wider public, prompted action, as the death toll rose. The government belatedly started to recommend social distancing, and closed schools, but Johnson did not announce a national lockdown until March 23. In the following months, testimony from NHS staff, and patients, showed that hospitals – already struggling, due to underfunding during a decade of austerity – had to deal with an additional crisis. There was a shortage of ventilators, despite claims by the government that they were urgently arranging to increase production and acquisition, while many frontline health workers lacked the required Personal Protective Equipment (PPE). The UK rapidly suffered one of the largest Covid death totals, per head of population, in the world, and this continued to be the case for many months.

In late May, it was revealed that Dominic Cummings, the chief advisor to Johnson, plus the former's wife, Mary Wakefield, had deliberately broken lockdown, while they were both ill with Covid, taking a trip from London to Durham. Wakefield and Cummings had also published a false account, claiming that they stayed in London, self-isolating, while unwell. Despite widespread public anger, and political pressure, Johnson refused to dismiss Cummings. A few months later, Cummings departed from his role, having upset Carrie Symonds, who was Johnson's partner, and a person with a disproportionately large influence in a power struggle within Downing Street. Lockdown eased over the late Spring and Summer, with pubs and restaurants re-opening, and schools returned to normal in September. This all caused a rise in Covid cases, to which the government reacted with a delayed second lockdown, lasting four weeks, from early November to the start of December. Post-Brexit negotiations, between the UK government and the EU, took place at intervals during the transition period. An agreement was finally announced on Christmas Eve, following which Parliament approved legislation on December 30, and the European Union (Future Relationship) Act 2020 received Royal Assent on the last day of a tumultuous year.

Johnson announced a third lockdown, on January 4 2021, as the numbers of Covid cases, and deaths, moved towards a peak higher than in the first wave, the previous Spring. Throughout the pandemic, the government displayed a grotesque combination of incompetence and corruption. Co-ordination of the national test and trace system was outsourced to Serco, a private company, rather than being led by the NHS. Edward Argar, a government Health minister, was a former executive at Serco. The current chief executive, Rupert Soames, was the brother of Nicholas Soames, a recently-retired Conservative MP. The Serco system failed to be effective, despite a massive budget, increased to £37 billion in March 2021. The government also awarded hundreds of multi-million pound contracts for the procurement of PPE. Many deals were agreed with companies, lacking experience with PPE, run by people who were donors to the Conservatives, or friends of the party's MPs. In an attempt to conceal the extent of the scandal, Matt Hancock delayed publication of the contracts, which led to a High Court ruling, during February 2021, that he had acted unlawfully. A year on from the initial fatalities, the Covid death total in the UK reached 126,000 people during March, based on the government's preferred measure, which was a death within 28 days of a positive test. A more realistic record showed a higher figure, as over 149,000 people had Covid recorded as a cause on their death certificate.

Covid restrictions were gradually eased in the Spring, while the government continued to give mixed messages. Border control had been haphazard throughout the pandemic, and there was now a delay of several weeks in limiting travel from India, where cases were particularly high, as Johnson sought a trade deal with the authoritarian government of that state. This led to a large number of British cases of the Delta Variant, first identified in India. At the end of June, it emerged that Matt Hancock was having an affair with Gina Coladangelo, a long-term friend, who had been appointed a director at the Department of Health and Social Care a few months earlier. Johnson accepted Hancock's apology for breaking workplace social distancing rules, with security video from Hancock's office showing him kissing Coladangelo. Amidst much criticism, Hancock resigned from the government, the day after Johnson failed to dismiss him. On July 5, Johnson announced the end of Covid protections would happen a fortnight later.

Covid cases rose sharply during the final weeks of 2021, with the arrival of the Omicron variant, and the government restored some public health measures. Reports surfaced of multiple parties in Downing Street, during the course of the pandemic, which had broken restrictions on social gatherings. A video from a year earlier, in which members of Johnson's staff joked about a Christmas party, was broadcast on television. On the following day, December 8 2021, Johnson told Parliament "I have been repeatedly assured since these allegations emerged that there was no party, and that no Covid rules were broken". Johnson announced that the Cabinet Secretary, Simon Case, would investigate. Ten days later, Case was taken off the case, as he had attended one of a growing number of Whitehall parties being probed. The inquiry was passed to Sue Gray, another senior civil servant.

The Metropolitan Police refused several times to open a criminal investigation, but changed their mind in late January 2022, saying that 12 of the 16 events identified by Gray, across 2020 and 2021, may have broken the law. With the police persuading Gray to limit the detail in her report, an interim summary was published, on January 31. It was clear there had been multiple breaches of Covid rules in Downing Street, which meant the Prime Minister, who attended several parties, lied to Parliament in his attempted denial. Johnson, characteristically claiming he had not done anything wrong, refused calls for his resignation.

On April 12, it was announced that Boris Johnson and Rishi Sunak, the Chancellor of the Exchequer, had been fined for breaking Covid laws, along with Carrie Johnson, the wife of the premier. This was due to their attending a birthday celebration for Boris Johnson, at Downing

Street, in 2020. This was the first time a sitting Prime Minister had been found to have broken the criminal law (less than three years after Johnson's prorogation of Parliament was ruled unlawful). The Metropolitan Police concluded their investigation the following month, with 126 fines having been issued to 83 people, in respect of eight events. Although Johnson attended several of the illegal parties, he was not given any further fines.

A revised report from Sue Gray, released on May 25, was very critical of the political, and civil service, leadership in Downing Street, for allowing numerous law-breaking parties to be held. Johnson dishonestly claimed the report vindicated his explanation that he had been attending work events, to thank colleagues, as part of his leadership role. In the next few days, a growing number of Conservative MPs called for a vote of no confidence in Johnson as party leader. A vote was held on June 6, with Johnson winning by a margin of 211 votes to 148. The size of the rebellion was larger than that experienced by Theresa May in a 2018 vote, but Johnson's supporters were willing to keep an obviously weak Prime Minister in power. With the Conservative government having abandoned measures to counter the pandemic, during February, the number of people who had died from Covid, based on death certificates, had now tragically risen to nearly 196,000. The United Kingdom had the highest Covid death total in Europe.

Little more than a fortnight after Johnson won the vote of confidence from Conservative colleagues, the party lost two By-Elections, following the departure of MPs due to sexual misconduct. This prompted the resignation of Oliver Dowden, as Party Chairman and a Cabinet Minister. A week later, Christopher Pincher, the Deputy Chief Whip, resigned amidst more allegations of improper sexual activity. The next few days saw dishonest denials from Johnson, and his allies, about knowledge of past actions by Pincher. On July 5, Sajid Javid and Rishi Sunak resigned from the Cabinet, with criticisms of Johnson's leadership. The following day brought numerous resignations from government posts, as Conservative MPs called on Johnson to resign. On July 7, with over 50 government ministers and aides having resigned, Boris Johnson announced his decision to stand down as Prime Minister.

A Conservative leadership contest began a few days later. When the result of the final stage was announced, Liz Truss beat Rishi Sunak, in a vote of party members, by a margin of 57 per cent to 43 per cent. On the following day, September 6, Johnson and Truss travelled to Balmoral Castle, in Scotland, the Summer holiday home of Elizabeth II, for their respective resignation and appointment meetings with the monarch. Just two days after Liz Truss became Prime Minister, Queen Elizabeth suddenly died, at the age of 96, and Charles III became the monarch.

Kwasi Kwarteng, the Chancellor of the Exchequer, and closest political ally of Liz Truss, produced a mini budget, with massive tax cuts for the wealthiest people in Britain, to be funded by increased government borrowing. This provoked an adverse reaction in financial markets, with Sterling quickly dropping to its lowest rate against the Dollar since 1985. Three weeks after the mini budget, Truss sacked Kwarteng, blaming him for the collapse of the strategy they had agreed. On October 20 – with many Tory MPs in revolt against their new leader – Liz Truss announced her decision to resign as Prime Minister, only 44 days after being appointed. Truss said she would remain in post until a new Conservative Party leader was elected, with this scheduled for the following week. Boris Johnson flew back to a disunited kingdom, from a holiday in the Dominican Republic – taken during Parliamentary term time – in a vain attempt to regain the Tory leadership, and premiership. Johnson soon claimed he had the required hundred MP nominations to be on the ballot, but would not be putting his name forward. Rishi Sunak, the only candidate with a hundred nominations, was declared the winner, without the planned ballots of the Tory MPs and membership.

Rishi Sunak was appointed Prime Minister, by King Charles, on October 25. Sunak was the fifth Conservative Prime Minister during their twelve years in power. This was an echo of the four Tory premiers between 1951 and 1964. Arriving at 10 Downing Street, Sunak announced "This government will have integrity, professionalism, and accountability at every level". A few hours later, Sunak showed he did not mean this, re-appointing Suella Braverman to the role of Home Secretary, just six days after her resignation for breaking the Ministerial Code. Two weeks into the Sunak premiership, Gavin Williamson departed from the Tory Cabinet, for the third time in three and a half years, having been accused of bullying several MPs. Moving into 2023, Nadhim Zahawi, the Conservative Party Chairman, and Dominic Raab, the Deputy Prime Minister, both left the Cabinet, after investigations into misconduct.

The coronation of Charles III took place on May 6 2023. Many people enjoyed the historic ceremony, but there was growing disillusionment with the veneration of an unelected head of state. This symbolised a nation in thrall to its past, failing to build a modern democracy. The king's declarations included:

I Charles do solemnly and sincerely in the presence of God profess, testify, and declare that I am a faithful Protestant, and that I will, according to the true intent of the enactments which secure the Protestant succession to the throne, uphold and maintain the said enactments to the best of my powers according to law.

The idea that only Protestant members of a royal family, established by Egbert of Wessex, twelve hundred years earlier, could be head of state, in contemporary Britain, conflicted with the ideals of meritocracy, and equality, among all religious and secular communities.

The coronation of Charles was attended by Sunak, plus all seven of the growing group of ex-Prime Ministers, namely Major, Blair, Brown, Cameron, May, Johnson, and Truss. A few weeks earlier, on March 22, Boris Johnson had been questioned, for several hours, by the House of Commons Privileges Committee, over his statements to Parliament in response to the Partygate scandal. On June 9, Boris Johnson announced he was standing down as an MP, with immediate effect, having learned the outcome of the investigation. At this point, over 227,000 people in the United Kingdom had died from Covid, mostly during the premiership of Johnson. The report arrived on June 15, concluding Johnson had repeatedly, and deliberately, lied to Parliament, while showing contempt for the inquiry process. The committee said, if he had not already resigned, their recommendation would be to suspend Johnson for 90 days. The report was endorsed by the full House of Commons four days later, with 354 MPs supporting it, and just seven of them voting against. The downfall of Johnson, a man clearly not fit to be Prime Minister, echoed that of Anthony Eden, following the 1956 Suez crisis, and Neville Chamberlain, after the appeasement era of the 1930s.

With their economic policy failing, an increasingly authoritarian Conservative government clamped down on public protest, and trade union rights. They also tried to distract the public, with a culture war narrative, attacking modern British values, and ramping up hostility towards desperate asylum seekers, fleeing from persecution abroad. This was done despite Sunak and Braverman being born into families of Indian origin, which migrated to Britain, via east Africa, in the 1960s. Britain is a society of immigrants, which has been built, across the ages, by the arrival of Neolithic people, Celts, Romans, Anglo-Saxons, Vikings, Normans, Dutch, and Germans. In recent decades, people from the Commonwealth, and continental Europe, have added to the process, enabling Britain to become an increasingly diverse, multicultural, society. In uncertain times, millions of people see the positive elements of British history as a cause for celebration, and hope for the future.

Printed in Great Britain
by Amazon